The Life of
the Hummingbird

THE Life of the

a Vineyard Book

Hummingbird

by ALEXANDER F. SKUTCH

Illustrated by ARTHUR B. SINGER

CROWN PUBLISHERS, INC.   New York

FOREWORD

OF ALL THE FAMILIES OF BIRDS, hummingbirds are perhaps the most unique. On the smallest of avian bodies, they bear the most glittering plumage and some of the most elegant adornments. By their beauty, intense activity, and association with bright flowers, they fascinate all who know them. For well over a century, we have had a succession of books on this single family, each outstanding in a different way. John Gould's sumptuous volumes of hand-colored plates, published in England in the middle of the last century, contain by far the most complete visual representation of the family that has ever appeared. Robert Ridgway's monograph of 1891 contains valuable descriptions of structure, along with a survey of what was then known of Hummingbirds' behavior. Among newer books, Crawford H. Greenewalt's is outstanding for its analysis of the flight and coloration of hummingbirds, while Walter Scheithauer's adds much to our understanding of their diet. Both are illustrated by superb color photographs.

The aim of the present book is a balanced and comprehensive account of hummingbirds: their appearance and structure, where they live, how they fly, what they eat, their relations with flowers, their temperament, how they court and build their nests and rear their young, their enemies, their future prospects. In preparing the text, the author has profited not only by earlier books but likewise by many recent papers, mostly published in scientific journals, which throw much new light on the physiology and behavior of these remarkable birds. These writings, to the authors of which he is greatly indebted, are listed in the bibliography at the back of the book. Moreover, he has enjoyed the immense advantage of over forty years' study of hummingbirds in their native homes in tropical America, and has probably watched more kinds of free hummingbirds at their nests than any other naturalist.

While planning the illustrations for this work, the artist, Arthur B. Singer, and the author spent some time together on a Costa Rican farm where hummingbirds abound, and where the former could watch some of his subjects as they went about their daily affairs. These illustrations, by one of the world's foremost delineators of birds, depict aspects of hummingbird behavior that have not yet been captured in photographs.

I wish to express my deep sense of obligation to Dr. Oliver L. Austin, Jr. of the University of Florida, whose counsel and advice in the organization of the manuscript proved invaluable.

A.F.S.

1973 by Vineyard Books, Inc., New York

All rights reserved. No part of this publication may be reproduced, stored in a retrieval system, or transmitted, in any form or by any means, electronic, mechanical, photocopying, recording, or otherwise, without the prior written permission of the publisher.

Library of Congress Catalogue Card Number: 73-815-14
ISBN: 0-517-50572-X
Printed in Italy by A. Mondadori, Verona

Contents

THE FAMILY TREE OF BIRDS

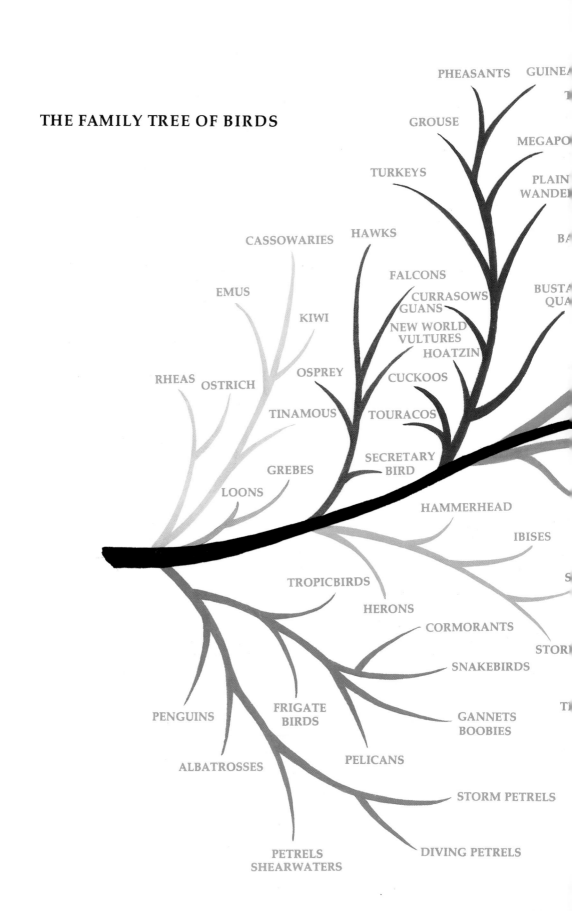

PHEASANTS GUINEA
GROUSE
MEGAPO
TURKEYS
PLAIN
WANDE
CASSOWARIES HAWKS
BA
FALCONS
EMUS
CURRASOWS
GUANS
KIWI
NEW WORLD
VULTURES
BUSTA
QUA
RHEAS OSTRICH OSPREY HOATZIN
CUCKOOS
TINAMOUS TOURACOS
SECRETARY
BIRD
GREBES
LOONS
HAMMERHEAD
IBISES
TROPICBIRDS S
HERONS
CORMORANTS
STORI
SNAKEBIRDS
FRIGATE T
PENGUINS BIRDS GANNETS
BOOBIES
PELICANS
ALBATROSSES
STORM PETRELS
DIVING PETRELS
PETRELS
SHEARWATERS

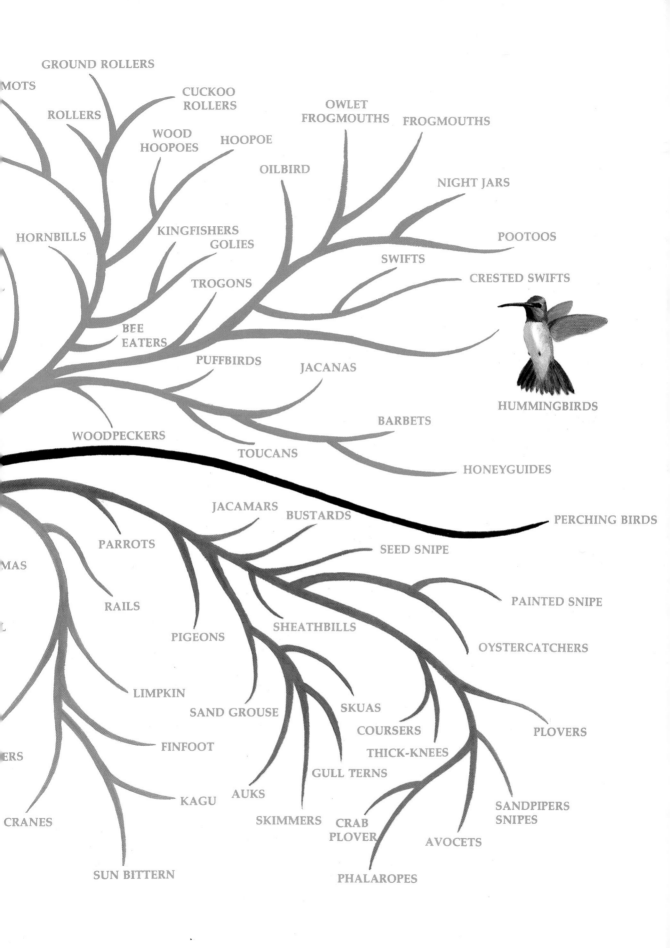

GROUND ROLLERS

MOTS

CUCKOO
ROLLERS

ROLLERS

OWLET
FROGMOUTHS

FROGMOUTHS

WOOD
HOOPOES

HOOPOE

OILBIRD

NIGHT JARS

HORNBILLS

KINGFISHERS
GOLIES

POOTOOS

SWIFTS

CRESTED SWIFTS

TROGONS

BEE
EATERS

PUFFBIRDS

JACANAS

BARBETS

HUMMINGBIRDS

WOODPECKERS

TOUCANS

HONEYGUIDES

JACAMARS

BUSTARDS

PERCHING BIRDS

PARROTS

SEED SNIPE

MAS

PAINTED SNIPE

RAILS

SHEATHBILLS

PIGEONS

OYSTERCATCHERS

LIMPKIN

SKUAS

SAND GROUSE

COURSERS

PLOVERS

FINFOOT

THICK-KNEES

ERS

GULL TERNS

KAGU

AUKS

CRANES

SKIMMERS

CRAB
PLOVER

AVOCETS

SANDPIPERS
SNIPES

SUN BITTERN

PHALAROPES

Chimborazo Hillstar
(*Oreotrochilus chimborazo*)
Ecuador

Bearded Helmetcrest
(*Oxypogon guerinii*)
Venezuela, Colombia

Bearded Mountaineer
(*Oreonympha nobilis*)
Peru

The Hummingbird Family

What is more gentle than a wind in summer?
What is more soothing than the pretty hummer
That stays one moment in an open flower,
And buzzes cheerily from bower to bower?

So wrote John Keats in 1816. Hummingbirds, which are confined to the Western Hemisphere and were unknown in Europe before the voyages of Columbus, had long since become familiar to cultured Europeans, so the poet could assume that his readers would understand his abbreviated reference to an exotic bird. Yet in the new world discovered by Columbus were many birds that rivaled the hummingbirds in splendor while far exceeding them in size, whose habits were certainly no less interesting, but that remained—and still remain—unknown to the general public not only of Europe but of America itself. How, then, can we explain the strong appeal of hummingbirds?

Undoubtedly they owe their fame to their extreme smallness no less than to their exquisite glittering plumage and unrivaled skill in flight. The superlatively small, like the superlatively large, ever captures our imagination. And the hummingbird family (Trochilidae) includes not only some of the smallest of birds but also the smallest of warm-blooded animals. The distinction of being the tiniest bird in the world belongs to the bee hummingbird[1] of Cuba, nearly half of whose length of two and a quarter inches is contributed by its bill and tail. Hummingbirds of middle size are about as large and heavy as the smallest American flycatchers, while the colossus of the family, the giant hummingbird of the Andes,

---

[1]The scientific names of hummingbirds are given in the index.

Giant Hummingbird (*Patagona gigas*)
Western South America from Ecuador to Chile

The smallest of all birds is the bee hummingbird, only
2½ inches long. The largest hummingbird is the giant
hummingbird, 8½ inches in length.

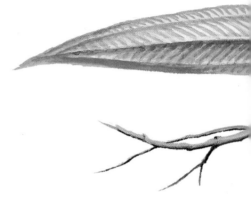

measures eight and a half inches, which is about the length of a starling
or an American catbird. The bee weighs less than two grams (about one-
fifteenth of an ounce); the giant, about twenty grams.

Another reason for the hummingbirds' popularity is the prompt
acceptance by certain species, of the conditions created by human settle-
ment. Let a man plant a flower garden almost anywhere from Canada
to Argentina and Chile, in the lowlands or mountains, amid humid forests
or in irrigated deserts, and before long his bright blossoms will be visited
by a tiny, glittering creature that hovers before them with wings vibrated
into twin halos while it sucks their sweet nectar. Most of the larger birds
whose brilliance should make them famous are, as they are often pursued
by man, far more retiring.

Such acceptance of man and his alterations of the environment, of
course, would make hummingbirds familiar only to the people of their
homeland in the New World. But they have other qualities, less fortunate
for themselves, which brought them wide renown beyond the sea: their
minute size and gemlike appearance caused them to be coveted as jewelry

Bee Hummingbird
(*Mellisuga helenae*)
Cuba

and adornments for women's hats. Early in the nineteenth century they became an important article in the commerce between Europe and tropical America. In one year, a single London dealer imported more than 400,000 skins from the West Indies alone. A principal source of these dried hummingbirds was Colombia, where some of the most lovely species live. Keeping a keen eye on this vast flow of desiccated birds from little-known lands, the cabinet naturalists of Europe detected and described many hitherto unknown species, often naming them for men or women whom they admired or wished to flatter. In this way, many birds of the republican Americas came to bear the names of European princes and noblemen. It is uncertain whether the slaughter of countless millions of hummingbirds for export caused the extermination of any species; but a few are known only from these old trade skins and have not been seen by naturalists in their native homes, perhaps remote Andean valleys.

The approximately 8,700 species of living birds fall into two great groups of almost equal size, one of which ornithologists distinguish as the passerines, a single order including the songbirds, the American flycatchers,

11

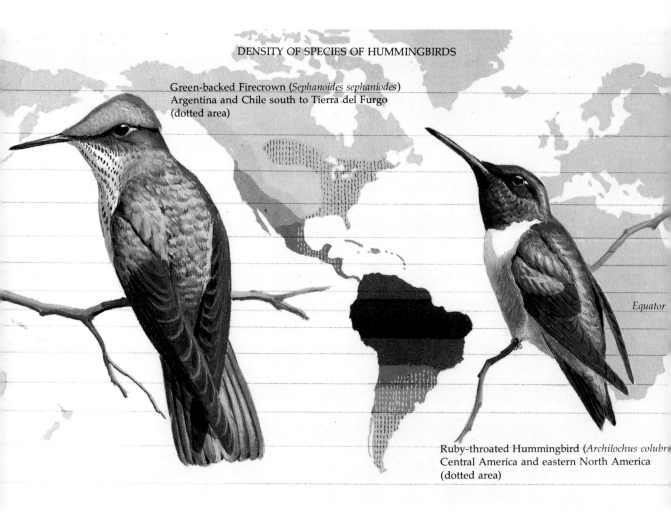

Green-backed Firecrown (*Sephanoides sephaniodes*)
Argentina and Chile south to Tierra del Furgo
(dotted area)

Equator

Ruby-throated Hummingbird (*Archilochus colubri*
Central America and eastern North America
(dotted area)

and a number of families that are less familiar. The remaining twenty-eight orders of the avian class, ranging in size from ostriches to hummingbirds and including parrots, pigeons, and pheasants, are for convenience lumped together as the nonpasserines. Hummingbirds were for a long while united with swifts in the order Apodiformes. The most obvious characteristic that these two families share is superb power of flight, associated with a peculiar anatomy of the wings in which the part corresponding to our arms is greatly abbreviated, while that which represents the human hand is highly developed and carries by far the larger surface of flight feathers.

Even in their manner of flight, however, hummingbirds and swifts differ greatly. The former have great maneuverability, being able to fly backward or sideward as well as to hover motionless, but they do not ordinarily stay in the air for long intervals. Swifts do not appear capable of all the hummingbirds' aerobatic feats, but they commonly remain aloft for extended periods, dashing and circling high above the treetops in pursuit of insects. Even where they are numerous, one rarely sees them at rest. Indeed, there is good circumstantial evidence that one species, the common swift of Europe, passes whole nights in the air, evidently taking whatever rest it needs. Moreover, swifts, with their dusky plumage, are among the drabbest of birds, whereas hummingbirds are the most brilliant. Swifts regularly pair, and both sexes perform all the duties of the nest; while pairing is exceptional among hummingbirds, and as a rule, only the females care for the eggs and young.

In view of these and other differences, certain recent classifiers have placed the hummingbird family in an order of its own, the Trochiliformes. And they have set this order, with its single family, at the very head of the nonpasserines, just below the passerines, as the most highly evolved of the twenty-eight nonpasserine orders. This place of honor has usually been assigned to the woodpeckers, another highly specialized and fascinating family of birds. The ancestry of hummingbirds remains in doubt, as their fragile, aerial bodies are not likely to become fossils and the geological record does not enlighten us. That the family is ancient is attested by its many species and wide dispersion over the Western Hemisphere, where doubtless it originated.

With 320 species in 123 genera, the hummingbird family is the largest in this hemisphere, with the single exception of the American flycatchers, of which 367 species are known. The center of abundance of the hummingbird family is the equatorial belt, ten degrees wide, across South America, where more than half of the species are found. Let it not be inferred from this that all hummingbirds are delicate creatures, unable to withstand a touch of frost. Quite the contrary, some are extremely hardy; equatorial South America could not boast so many kinds if it did not include the high Andes of Ecuador, Colombia, and Peru, with their dazzling array of species, many of which dwell at altitudes where the temperature of the thin atmosphere quickly falls to the freezing point after the sun sets. The hardiest of all reach heights exceeding 15,000 feet, on the verge of the perennial snowfields of Chimborazo, Cotopaxi, Sangay, and other sublime Andean peaks.

From the equatorial zone the number of kinds of hummingbirds gradually decreases toward the north and south. Costa Rica's 20,000 square

Ruby-throated Hummingbird leaves the inhospitable climate of eastern North America for Central America in winter.

Ruby-throated Hummingbird
(*Archilochus colubris*)
Central America and eastern North America

miles of mountainous terrain supports fifty-four species. Mexico, over thirty times as large, has only fifty-one species. In the western United States, thanks to the continuity of its mountain chains with those of tropical and subtropical Mexico, twelve species breed. The vast extent of the United States east of the Mississippi and eastern Canada, more isolated from the center of abundance of hummingbirds in the tropics, has only one species, the rubythroat. Although thirteen kinds of hummingbirds breed in the continental United States, only four do in Canada. And only one species reaches the Strait of Magellan.

Unlike some of the other large avian families that evidently arose in South America, such as the antbirds and manakins, hummingbirds have not clung closely to the mainland and islands almost within sight of it but have colonized more distant islands. They have spread throughout

14

Rufous Hummingbird migrates all the way from northwestern North America to Mexico.

Rufous Hummingbird
(*Selasphorus rufus*)
Western North America

the West Indies and the Bahamas, where nineteen species occur. Two species have become established in the tiny Juan Fernández group, in the Pacific 400 miles from the Chilean coast. One of these, the Chilean firecrown, is widely distributed on the South American mainland; the other, known as the Juan Fernández hummingbird, is endemic to this archipelago, where it has been present so long that it has become differentiated into two well-marked races on islands 100 miles apart.

Hummingbirds owe their wide distribution to their great power of flight and wandering habits no less than to their hardiness. On the Costa Rican farm where I write, some species, including the lovely white-necked Jacobin, appear only at long intervals, become abundant, then mysteriously vanish. They are not known to be long-distance migrants and their journeys have not been traced, but they evidently wander widely in search

15

of abundant flowers. Other hummingbirds, such as the green violet-ear, migrate altitudinally, ascending the mountains to nest in the flowery season, then dropping lower to avoid the wet season's chilling rains. Anna's hummingbird of California does just the opposite, breeding at low elevations early in the year, then often moving upward to flower-spangled mountain meadows.

Among the long-distance migrants are the ruby-throated hummingbird, which breeds as far north as southern Canada and occasionally reaches western Panama in winter. Some rubythroats evidently cross the Gulf of Mexico, on a continuous flight of more than 500 miles. Of the several migratory hummingbirds in western North America, the greatest traveler is the rufous, which breeds from southern Oregon and Idaho to southeastern Alaska and in winter reaches the Mexican state of Guerrero, over 2,000 miles by an overland route from its nearest summer home—a prodigious journey for a birdling weighing only three or four grams. At the other extreme of hummingbird distribution, the Chilean firecrown breeds as far south as bleak Tierra del Fuego and migrates northward during the coldest months.

Colors and Adornments

THE NAMES THAT admiring naturalists have given to hummingbirds suggest exquisite, fairylike grace and gemlike refulgence. Fiery-tailed awlbill, ruby-topaz hummingbird, glittering-bellied emerald, blue-chinned sapphire, violet-capped woodnymph, gilded hummingbird, white-tailed goldenthroat, blossomcrown, Brazilian ruby, green-crowned brilliant, Andean hillstar, shining sunbeam, amethyst-throated sunangel, glowing puffleg, bronze-tailed comet, purple-crowned fairy, horned sungem, amethyst woodstar—these are a few of the colorful names that I find, not in a poet's vision of Elysian groves, but applied to some of the 233 species of hummingbirds briefly described in Meyer de Schauensee's scientific *Guide to the Birds of South America.*

One would expect his first glimpse of a creature that bears one of these glamorous names to be a breathtaking vision of beauty. Often he is disappointed. To behold the hummingbird's most vivid colors, he may have to wait patiently before flowers that it habitually visits, until it turns squarely toward the viewer. Then the gorget or the crown—usually the male hummingbird's most glittering parts—which at first appeared so lusterless, suddenly gleams with the most intense metallic green, blue, violet, magenta, or ruby, like a sunbeam suddenly breaking through a dark cloud. The fiery glitter is often all too brief, for with the first turn of the hummer's body it expires as suddenly as it flared up. How different

Iridescent colors are common among humming-birds. By changing position the direction of the reflected light might give the effect of two completely different colors of the same plumage parts.

from the bright colors of such birds as tanagers, orioles, and wood warblers, which are visible at a glance and show to almost equal advantage from any angle.

The colors of birds, including their many shades of red, orange, yellow, brown, gray, and black, are usually produced by pigments, which are likewise responsible for most of the colors of natural objects, such as flowers, and of human artifacts, including all painted surfaces and dyed fabrics. Pigments operate by absorbing certain of the wavelengths that make up white light and sending forth the rejected waves impartially in all directions, like a primary source of light, so that the hue of a pigmented body changes little with varying angles of vision.

In addition to pigments, colors may be produced by the structure of intrinsically colorless bodies. Such colors are typically iridescent, varying with the angle at which light falls upon them and with that from which they are viewed, as one sees in a soap bubble or a film of oil on water. Structural colors may be caused by the differential scattering of light of different wavelengths by minute particles, as in the blue sky and roseate sunset; by refraction, as when a prism spreads out white sunbeams into a colored spectrum; or by the combination of reflection and refraction,

This is illustrated in these two pictures of the same bird, a Ruby-topaz Hummingbird (*Chrysolampis mosquitus*) Northern South America

as in a rainbow. More complexly, structural colors may be caused by interference, which occurs when a train of light waves is reflected back on itself in such a way that the crest of one wave coincides with the trough of another of the same length and the two cancel each other's effect; only waves of other lengths remain effective to stimulate the eye and impart their color to the body.

Since light waves are so short, the phenomenon of interference is caused by exceedingly fine structures, such as thin films. We owe much of our understanding of the colors of hummingbirds to the researches of Crawford Greenewalt, who showed that beneath the surface of the minute divisions of a feather known as barbules there are, on the hummingbird's iridescent parts, tiny elliptical bodies arranged in the form of a mosaic. These bodies consist of stacks of filmlike platelets, which are not homogeneous, but are composed of air bubbles encased in a matrix of refractive index a little greater than two. Different colors are produced by differences in both the air content and the thickness of the platelets. By refracting and reflecting light waves, these exceedingly thin platelets cause interference.

As in other structural or iridescent colors, the effect upon the viewer

19

1.

2.

3.

4.

5.

depends on where he stands in relation to the object viewed and the source of light. On the hummingbirds's glittering throat or crown, the exposed surfaces of the barbules resemble tiny flat mirrors, which send forth their refulgence in one favored direction. Thus it happens that as the hummingbird turns aside, his scintillating gorget may change from red or violet to green or black. All the metallic colors of hummingbirds are caused by interference; but on the back of the body the outer surface of each barbule is concave instead of flat, and, like a curved mirror, it reflects light from the same source in many directions, so that the hummingbird's green back appears green from all sides. However, since the light is diffused rather than concentrated in one direction, the color is less intense. In other kinds of birds, blue is usually a structural color, while some greens are produced by the combined action of structural blue and yellow pigment. Hummingbirds' many shades of rufous, cinnamon, brown, and purplish black are due to pigment. They have no red or yellow pigment in their plumage.

Most hummingbirds owe their beauty to their graceful streamlined form and shining metallic colors. Their plumage, despite its glitter, is essentially utilitarian, consisting of feathers, in every particular not related to color,

LEFT TO RIGHT: 1. Violet-tailed Sylph (*Aglaiocercus coelestis*) Colombia, Ecuador; 2. Crimson Topaz (*Topaza pella*) Northeastern South America; 3. Wire-crested Thorntail (*Popelairia popelairii*) Colombia, Ecuador, Peru; 4. Tufted Coquette (*Lophornis ornata*) Northeastern South America; 5. Booted Racket-tail (*Ocreatus underwoodii*) Northwestern South America; 6. Horned Sungem (*Heliactin cornuta*) Brazil 7. Black-breasted Plovercrest (*Stephanoxis lalandi*) Brazil, Paraguay, Argentina; 8. Red-tailed Comet (*Sappho sparganura*) Bolivia, Argentina, Peru;

like those worn by even the plainest of small birds. In species without frills and ribbons, the female is often hard to distinguish from the male. A minority of hummingbirds have special adornments, usually in the form of expansible gorgets with projecting corners, crests on the head, elongated and variously modified tail feathers, or powder-puff thighs. As in other families of birds with extravagant adornments, these are usually confined to the male; the female would be incommoded by them while attending her nest.

One of the more familiar of the long-tailed hummingbirds is the green-and-black streamertail, the most abundant and widespread member of the family on the island of Jamaica, where it is often called the "doctor bird." Incidentally, this bird, known to scientists as *Trochilus polytmus*, is the name-bearer of the whole hummingbird family, the Trochilidae. The next-to-outermost feather on each side of the male's tail is six or seven inches long, far longer than its bearer's body. Trailing behind the flying hummingbird like thin black streamers, these feathers make a humming sound.

Among the few North American hummingbirds with very long tails are the sheartails of Guatemala and Mexico. The slender sheartail of the

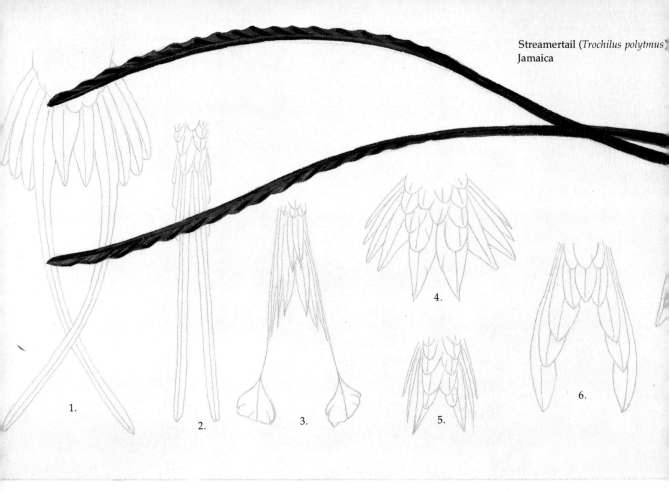

1.
2.
3.
4.
5.
6.

1. Crimson Topaz (*Topaza pella*) Northeastern South America
2. Peruvian Sheartail (*Thaumastura cora*) Peru
3. Racket-tailed Coquette (*Discosura longicauda*) Northeastern South America
4. Allen's Hummingbird (*Selasphorus sasin*) California
5. White-bellied Woodstar (*Acestrura mulsant*) Colombia, Ecuador, Peru, Bolivia

Guatemalan highlands is a small, bronzy-green hummingbird with, in the male, a bright metallic violet gorget and a deeply forked tail longer than his body and bill together. I was delighted to meet this unusual hummingbird amid flowery thickets near the shore of Lake Atitlán, where I heard it called the "quetzalito"—the little quetzal. If it were as big as Guatemala's national bird, it might be equally renowned.

In South America, where the most gorgeous hummingbirds are most abundant, long-tailed species are more numerous. The male red-tailed comet of the Bolivian Andes has a very long, deeply forked, graduated tail, of which the broad feathers, lying one above the other like the shingles of a roof, are shining reddish-gold, each tipped with dusky purple. The equally prominent tail of the male long-tailed sylph, a species widespread in the tropical Andes, is glittering purple, blue, or green.

22   Most curious is the tail of the marvelous spatuletail, a rare species

7.

8.

9.

10.

11.

6. Natterer's Emerald (*Ptochoptera iolaima*) Brazil
7. Amethyst Woodstar (*Calliphlox amethystina*) South America
8. White-necked Jacobin (*Florisuga mellivora*) Northern South America
9. Marvelous Spatuletail (*Loddigesia mirabilis*) Peru
10. Black-bellied Thorntail (*Popelairia langsdorffi*) Northern South America
11. Green-tailed Trainbearer (*Lesbia nuna*) Northwestern South America

restricted to part of a single valley in the Peruvian Andes. Each outermost tail feather consists of a long, bare shaft that curves first outward, then inward in a semicircle, to cross the shaft from the opposite side and terminate in a great, blackish purple racket that seems hardly to be connected with the diminutive hummingbird. The next pair of tail feathers from the outside are quite different, being long, straight, slender, and pointed. All the remaining tail feathers are rudimentary.

The male wire-crested thorntail, of the eastern slopes of the northern Andes, has elongated tail feathers that curve outward and taper from a broad base to a slender tip. The outermost is longest and each successive feather toward the center is shorter. All are steel-blue, with white shafts, making a most striking and curious display when spread. As its name implies, this elegant little thorntail has a crest of brilliant green feathers, the longest of which stand up above the crown like thin wires, reminding

23

1. Rivoli's Hummingbird (*Eugenes fulgens*) U.S., Mexico
2. Gilded Hummingbird (*Hylocharis chrysura*) Southern Brazil and neighboring countries
3. Garnet-throated Hummingbird (*Lamprolaima rhami*) Northern Central America
4. Chimborazo Hillstar (*Oreotrochilus chimborazo*) Ecuador
5. Calliope Hummingbird (*Stellula calliope*) Canada, U.S., Mexico
6. Hooded Visorbearer (*Augastes lumachellus*) Brazil
7. Anna's Hummingbird (*Calypte anna*) U.S., Mexico
8. Rainbow-bearded Thornbill (*Chalcostigma herrani*) Colombia, Ecuador
9. Wire-crested Thorntail (*Popelairia popelairii*) Colombia, Ecuador, Peru
10. White-vented Violet-ear (*Colibri serrirostris*) Bolivia, Argentina, Brazil
11. Adorable Coquette (*Lophornis adorabilis*) Southern Central America

one of the European lapwing. Other crested hummingbirds are the horned sungem, the bearded helmetcrest, and the rainbow-bearded thornbill, the first Brazilian, the last two inhabitants of the high Andes.

The crested hummingbirds that the Northerner is most likely to meet are the coquettes, marvelous atoms of bird life that range, in their several species, from Bolivia to tropical Mexico. I still vividly recall my delight when, nearly four decades ago, I met one of these wonderful creatures in a Costa Rican coffee plantation, sipping nectar from the clustered white florets of an Inga shade tree. It was a male white-crested coquette, in perfect plumage, and so tame that he permitted me to examine him at arm's length while he perched low in a coffee bush between visits to the flowers. Never before had I seen so small a bird with such profuse adornment: a high, peaked, white crest standing above a coppery-bronze forehead; the brilliant green of his throat and cheeks extending into a long, slender tuft of green feathers on either side of his head, projecting far behind; a white chest, cinnamon-rufous abdomen, and (unusual in hummingbirds) a white band across the lower end of his metallic green back, separating it from his coppery-purple rump.

Let it not be inferred from these descriptions that every hummingbird, or at least every adult male, is a glittering gem. The most brilliant hummingbirds live chiefly where sunshine sets their splendors aglow. A large group, the so-called hermits, consists of long-billed species of generally brownish coloration that dwell in the dim undergrowth of tropi- cal forests and thickets, where their modest attire makes them difficult to detect when motionless. Yet these plainer hummingbirds are by no means devoid of embellishment. Many have subdued bronze-green backs. Rich shades of cinnamon or rufous color some of them, or striking tail patterns of black and white. Many have elongated, white-tipped central tail feathers.

One of the dullest of hummingbirds is the biggest, the brownish giant hummingbird of the southern Andes. One of the most curiously attired is the brown violet-ear, whose dull plumage is relieved only by the violet on the sides of the head and a patch of glittering green on the throat, evidently poor remnants of the more splendid dress worn by remote ancestors, as by contemporaries of the same genus. This strange hum- mingbird is thinly scattered from Guatemala to Bolivia.

Flight

THE FLIGHT OF HUMMINGBIRDS is no less wonderful than their refulgent plumage. Watch a hummingbird as it sucks nectar from a spike or panicle of long, tubular flowers pointing in all directions. Now it hovers motionless on wings vibrated into unsubstantial blurs, while its long bill probes the depths of a corolla. Its drink finished, it flies backward to withdraw its bill from the tube, hovers briefly, then perhaps shifts sideways in the air, to place itself squarely in front of another blossom. With equal facility it adjusts its level up or down to reach higher or lower flowers. If the flower points sideward, the bird hovers with its body only slightly inclined; if it points downward, the hummingbird with equal ease drinks with its hovering body nearly vertical and its bill directed straight up. When it has satisfied its thirst, it may pivot around on a fixed point in the air before it darts swiftly away.

Although heavier than air, the hummingbird appears to be in perfect equilibrium with it, like a fish in water; with equal ease it moves in any direction, forward or backward, up or down, to the right or to the left, as well as pivoting on a stationary axis. No other bird can do all these things. The only limitation to the hummingbird's competence in the air is its inability to soar on motionless wings; this is a capacity reserved for larger birds with broader wings.

Among the hummingbird's other accomplishments is its ability to achieve practically full speed at the instant it takes wing. Indeed, it has been said to start flying before it leaves its perch; far from using the perch as a resistance against which to push with its feet and spring forward, it may lift a slender twig slightly at the moment of leaving it. Similarly, it has no need to reduce velocity as it approaches a perch; it may reach the perch at full speed and stop abruptly, in a way that would be disastrous to an airplane or a heavier bird.

Some of the hummingbird's flying abilities are useful not only when visiting flowers but also while nesting. Certain hummingbirds, notably the hermits, fasten their nest beneath the arching tip of a palm leaf, which they always face while incubating eggs or brooding nestlings. To leave, they start beating their wings while still sitting, fly upward and backward until clear of nest and leaf, then reverse and dart away. To return to the nest, hummingbirds of all kinds fly right into it instead of alighting on the rim or nearby and hopping in, as other birds do. By the time the newly arrived hummingbird's wings are folded, it is already incubating. When a white-eared hummingbird wishes to change her orientation in the nest, she sets her wings in motion, rises up slightly, and pivots around. When she wishes to turn her eggs, she flies upward and backward about one inch, to alight on the rim facing inward.

Another remarkable feat of the hummingbird is flying upside-down. If suddenly assailed from the front, as while visiting a flower, it may turn a backward somersault by flipping its spread tail forward, dart a short distance with its wings in reverse and feet upward, then roll over and continue in normal flight.

To understand how a hummingbird can do all these things, we must consider the structure of its flying apparatus, especially the wings and the muscles that move them. As already mentioned when comparing

Anatomy of the wing of a pelican (left) and of a hummingbird (right)

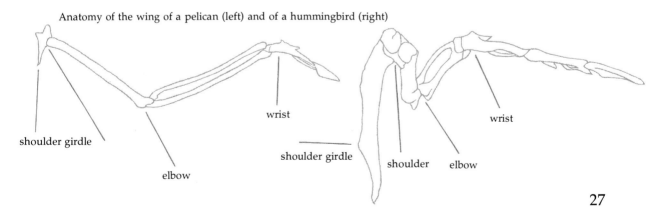

shoulder girdle

wrist

elbow

shoulder girdle

shoulder

elbow

wrist

27

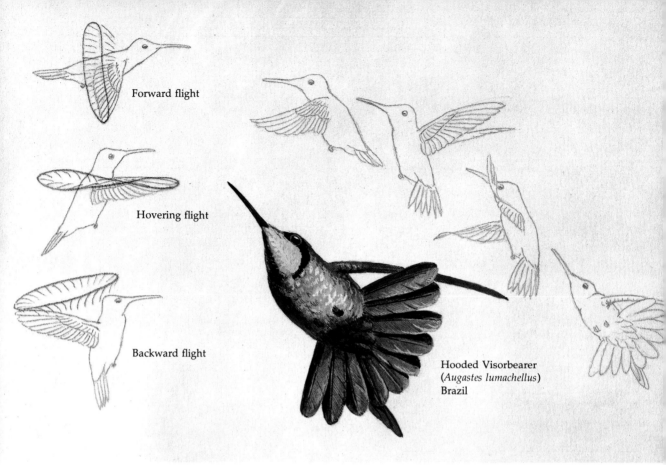

Forward flight

Hovering flight

Backward flight

Hooded Visorbearer
(*Augastes lumachellus*)
Brazil

Sequence shows backward somersault as hummingbird makes a getaway.

hummingbirds and swifts, the wings of both are practically all "hand," the part that corresponds to our arms being greatly reduced in size. The hummingbird's hand bears ten large flight feathers, known as primaries, but the forearm bears only six or seven such feathers, called secondaries—whereas a soaring bird, such as the albatross, has ten primaries and about forty secondaries.

The hummingbird's short arm bones form a rigid V· the elbow and wrist joints allow little flexure. The shoulder joint, on the contrary, is extremely supple, permitting not only movement in all directions but also axial rotation of the whole wing through about 180 degrees. (Our own shoulder joint permits us to swing our arms about as freely as a hummingbird moves its wings, but permits only slight axial rotation of the whole arm; although some of us can revolve our hands through nearly 360 degrees, the forearm does most of the rotation.) The concentration of the wings' weight near the base where the larger bones are situated facilitates changes in their position relative to the hummingbird's body.

The hummingbird has a relatively large breastbone with a prominent keel. The muscles attached to it that move the wings are exceedingly

28

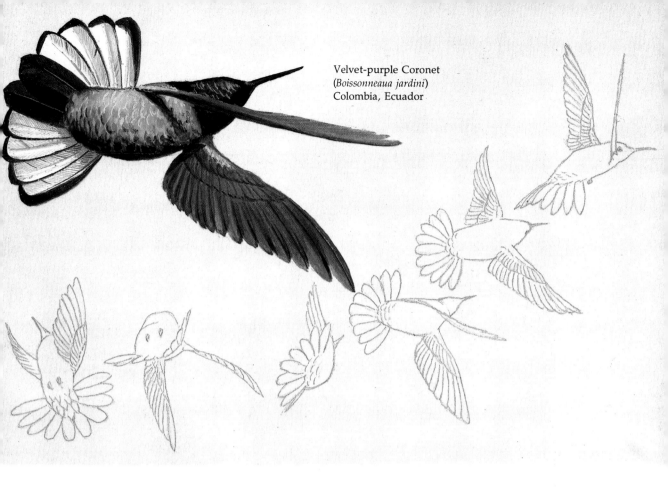

Velvet-purple Coronet
(*Boissonneaua jardini*)
Colombia, Ecuador

well developed, accounting for 25 or 30 per cent of the bird's weight. Moreover, the elevator muscles, which lift the wing, are about half as heavy as the depressor muscles, whose contraction makes the downstroke. In most birds the elevator muscles are only from one-tenth to one-twentieth as heavy as the depressor muscles.

These structural peculiarities give the hummingbird its exceptional control of all its movements in the air. In other birds only the downstroke gives lift or propulsion, the upstroke, made with the wings partly folded and the primaries separated to diminish air resistance, is a movement of recovery made with weak muscles, unavoidable, but contributing little to the bird's progress. In hummingbirds, on the contrary, both strokes are made with rigidly extended wings moved by powerful muscles. By altering the angle at which the wings cleave the air, both strokes are made to provide lift and propulsion.

When the hummingbird hovers motionless, its rapidly beating wings move forward and backward rather than up and down, their tips tracing a flat figure of eight in the air. With each reversal of the beat, the wings are pivoted through about 180 degrees, so that the front edge always

29

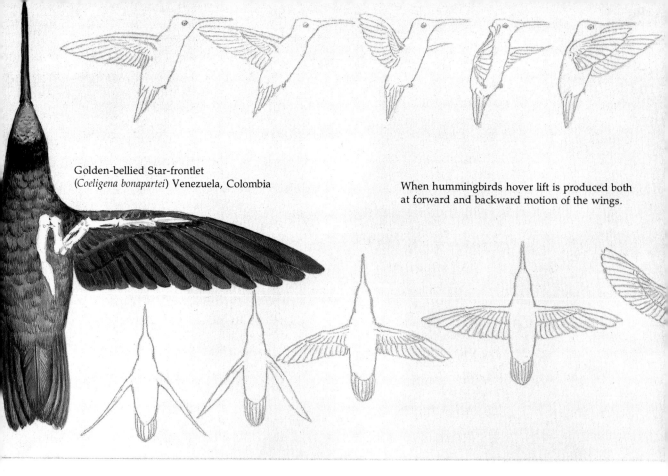

Golden-bellied Star-frontlet
(*Coeligena bonapartei*) Venezuela, Colombia

When hummingbirds hover lift is produced both
at forward and backward motion of the wings.

leads and on the backstroke the undersides of the flight feathers are uppermost. Accordingly, while both forward and back strokes give lift, they cancel whatever tendency to horizontal displacement each may have and hold the bird in a single spot with no evident oscillation.

The great majority of hummingbirds appear unable to walk or hop. They scarcely ever alight on the ground, and to move a few inches on a branch, they fly. They depend wholly upon their wings for locomotion.

The rate of the wingbeats that in many species make a humming sound is difficult to determine, as it is far too rapid to be followed by the human eye. The most accurate counts have been made while the hummingbird was hovering rather than flying forward, by using a stroboscope in a darkened room. This apparatus emits extremely brief, bright flashes of light at exceedingly short intervals. If it is exactly synchronized with the wingbeats, they will always be illuminated in the same position, so that the bird will appear to float on motionless wings. The rate of the flashes can then be read on the instrument's dial. Using this method on a variety of hummingbirds, Scheithauer obtained frequencies of from twenty-two to seventy-nine wingbeats per second, the complete cycle of a down and up stroke being counted as one beat. The slowest rates

Rufous Hummingbird
(*Selasphorus rufus*)
Western North America

were by the long-billed starthroat and the black-throated mango, large hummingbirds weighing respectively six and six and a half grams; the most rapid by the little white-bellied woodstar, which weighs only two and a half grams.

These results are in substantial agreement with those obtained earlier by C. H. Blake working with Harold Edgerton, by Crawford Greenewalt, and by other investigators. Just as a long pendulum swings more slowly than a short one, so a long wing beats more slowly than a short one. A mute swan's wing, twenty-eight inches long, flaps only one and a half times per second; a gnat's wing, a quarter of an inch in length, vibrates 500 times per second. Contrary to a prevalent impression, for their weight or wing length hummingbirds beat their wings less rather than more rapidly than other birds do. The giant hummingbird flaps only eight or ten times per second, whereas the much larger mockingbird does so about fourteen times. Many hummingbirds that weigh from five to seven grams flap at a rate of twenty to twenty-five times per second; but a chickadee, almost twice as heavy, beats its wings about twenty-seven times per second. Since only the chickadee's downstroke generates power, while both strokes of the hummingbird help to propel it, twenty-five 31 beats of a hummingbird evidently count for fifty of the chickadee or some other "ordinary" bird. The hummingbird can afford to flap its wings more slowly because there is no waste motion.

In courtship flights ruby-throated and rufous hummingbirds have been reported to beat their wings at the rate of 200 times per second.

At a given velocity, a small body appears to move faster than a large one—an optical illusion that is responsible for exaggerated claims of the speed of hummingbirds. A carefully controlled measurement of a hummingbird's velocity, made in a wind tunnel by Greenewalt, demonstrated that the top speed of a female rubythroat was 27 miles per hour. When the velocity of the air current passing through the tunnel was increased to 30 miles per hour, the bird tried vainly to reach the coveted syrup by flying against the current. Bees and wasps trying to reach the feeder in the same tunnel flew at a rate of scarcely more than 10 miles per hour. Augusto Ruschi observed flying speeds ranging from 14 to 25 miles per hour for several species of Brazilian hummingbirds on outdoor courses; he believed that none could exceed 30 miles per hour.

It appears, however, that under special conditions or with stronger motivation some kinds of hummingbirds can go faster. By taking motion pictures of an Allen's hummingbird diving earthward under wing power in courtship display, Oliver Pearson calculated its maximum velocity to be about 60 miles per hour. Using a stopwatch to time a male violet-ear's flight from one isolated tree to another, Helmuth Wagner found an average speed of over 56 miles per hour. In Scheithauer's indoor aviary, two long-tailed, or blue-throated, sylphs were in the habit of chasing each other, sometimes eight to twelve times without stopping, over a standard course, roughly a figure of eight, that led them through tropical vegetation and avoided enclosing walls. This course was about seventy-four yards long. By timing the birds repeatedly with a stopwatch, the aviculturist obtained velocities ranging from 30 to 47 miles per hour, with a mean of 38.4 miles per hour.

Although this speed may not impress people accustomed to jet travel, that a bird could hurtle so fast through obstructing vegetation in a small enclosed space, without dashing itself to death, reveals marvelously precise control of flight. And when we recall that songbirds, including those as large as thrushes, mostly fly at velocities between 20 and 35 miles per hour, and pigeons hardly go faster, the tiny hummingbird's performance commands admiration.

Food, Metabolism, and Longevity

MANY YEARS AGO I visited a house near the summit of a 10,000-foot Guatemalan mountain, where hummingbirds abounded. Urging me to eat more of his delicious high-altitude vegetables, my generous host remarked: "You have hardly eaten anything. You have an appetite like a hummingbird."

"It's fortunate," I replied, "that I do not have an appetite like a hummingbird. If I did, you might not invite me to visit you again. I would eat more than 300 pounds of food daily!"

The belief that a hummingbird can consume about twice its weight in sugar daily was due to the pioneer studies of Althea R. Sherman, who as early as 1907, in her dooryard in Iowa, trained free rubythroats to drink a solution of table sugar (sucrose) from a bottle placed in the center of an artificial flower. Soon she learned that her hummingbirds would visit bottles without an advertising corolla. They learned to associate her with her bounty, and if they found the bottles empty, they would hover around her until she filled one. Even after a year and a long migration, some remembered her.

By careful measurements Miss Sherman found that a single hummingbird consumed in one day syrup containing from 4.5 to 5.8 grams of sugar. For the weight of a hummingbird, she used that of a male who had blundered into a building and apparently died of starvation. The corpse's weight of 2.1 grams was substantially less than that of a living ruby-throated hummingbird, which others have found to be 2.9 to 3.5 grams. Hence an exaggerated statement of the relative weight of a hummingbird's daily ration that was widely quoted.

Years later, at a feeder in Colorado, Walker Van Riper found that a free female broad-tailed hummingbird, weighing 4.3 grams, drank each day from 7.1 to 10.6 grams of syrup containing 22 per cent of granulated white sugar. This bird took, on the average, twice her own weight of syrup but only 42 per cent of her weight in pure sugar—about a fifth of Miss Sherman's estimate. We do not know how much the broad-tail was eating away from the feeder.

When zoos and aviculturists tried to maintain hummingbirds on a sugary diet, the birds invariably died. This led to the the belief that hummingbirds visited flowers, not to sip their nectar, but to catch whatever small insects or spiders might be lurking within them. To prove the point, zoologists shot many hummingbirds and opened their stomachs—finding only minute insects and spiders in them. Hummingbirds, some concluded, were as insectivorous as any small flycatcher, and not dependent upon nectar. It apparently never occurred to them that nectar, with its readily absorbed sugars, passes almost immediately into the hummingbird's intestine, leaving the more slowly digested insects in the stomach. Why a largely or wholly insectivorous bird came so eagerly to feeders that offered only sugar-water remained unexplained. Perhaps these hummers had vitiated tastes!

To be convinced that the diet of hummingbirds consists of both nectar and insects, one does not have to watch them long in their natural habitat, especially in the tropics. They can be seen catching insects in the air or plucking them from foliage and twigs, and they persistently visit flowers where one will find few insects. To learn the relative proportions of sugars and proteins in a hummingbird's diet, however, one must keep it under controlled conditions, in an aviary or laboratory. Much light has been thrown on this matter by the admirable studies of Walter Scheithauer.

He began by isolating, in a glass-fronted box, a male white-ear in perfect health, who had already been in his aviary for six months. On the first trial the bird was offered only honey dissolved in water, with the addition of one drop of a vitamin preparation. In sixteen hours the white-ear drank 172 times, each drink continuing from one to eleven seconds, with an average length of five seconds. The longest interval between drinks, while the lights were on, was twelve minutes. The white-ear consumed

Racket-tailed Coquette
(*Discosura longicauda*)
Brazil and neighboring countries

Glittering-bellied Emerald
(*Chlorostilbon aureoventris*)
Brazil and neighboring countries

Swallow-tailed Hummingbird
(*Eupetomena macroura*)
Brazil and neighboring countries

35

2.5 grams of honey, which was 80 per cent of his own weight of 3 grams, and 25 grams of water, over eight times the bird's weight. Despite this enormous intake, he seemed unhappy. At first he searched for insects in the corners of the cage, but presently abandoned the fruitless effort. He ceased singing and yawned frequently; his eyes lost their brightness; by the day's end, he looked and acted unwell. On a diet of honey alone the hummingbird lost his vitality astonishingly fast.

Next the white-ear was given the same honey solution plus an unlimited supply of fruit flies, and the experiment was continued for six days. His average consumption in a sixteen-hour day was now 267 drinks lasting 3.5 seconds each, by which he imbibed 2.2 grams of honey, which was 73 per cent of his body weight. He caught and devoured an average of 677 fruit flies per day, which together weighed 0.8 gram, or 27 per cent of the bird's weight, and yielded rather less than 0.1 gram of protein. With both sugars and proteins available in unlimited quantities, the hummingbird still depended largely upon the carbohydrates for nourishment. And he remained in excellent condition, bright-eyed, active, singing, with glossy plumage.

Still further to test the white-ear's reactions to various foods, Scheithauer added egg yolk, mealworms, bovine blood serum, powdered milk, and bananas to the usual honey solution and blended the whole in a mixer, making a yellowish juice with a pleasant, rather sickly smell, which he gave to the bird along with living fruit flies. In sixteen hours the white-ear imbibed 25.6 grams of this concoction, or 856 per cent of his own weight in water and food, which included 2 grams of honey and 4 grams of other substances (fats, proteins, carbohydrates, etc.). At the day's end, the bird, who drank with the usual frequency but without his customary relish, looked tired and sick, "like a man who has celebrated too well and wants only to rest, sleep, and digest his heavy meal." The experimenter concluded that the hummingbird's principal need was sugar, and in trying to achieve his normal daily intake of 60 to 70 per cent of his body weight in honey, he ingested an excess of proteins and fats and made himself miserable.

Further experimentation showed that the food mixture the hummingbirds in the aviary had been receiving was too dilute. When 100 grams of food was served in more than 400 grams of water, none of the birds drank extra water. As the concentration of the mixture was increased beyond this point, they visited the water fountain more and more. As

Blue-tufted Starthroat (*Heliomaster furcifer*)
Central South America

a result of many tests Scheithauer adopted a food mixture consisting, in relation to the bird's body weight, of 400 per cent water, 70 per cent honey, 3 per cent protein, 2 per cent fat, and 6 per cent trace elements—minerals, vitamins, and roughage. These experiments also revealed the astonishing rapidity of the hummingbird's digestion. Ten minutes after the first fruit flies were eaten, their chitinous remains were voided.

That hummingbirds need much more nectar than insects is confirmed by observation in the field. Oliver Pearson spent two days recording every movement of a free male Anna's hummingbird in the botanical garden of the University of California at Berkeley. Averaging the records for the two days he found that the bird made 120 flights to flowers, devoting one hour and 53 minutes to nectar-feeding; but he spent only 4.5 minutes chasing insects, on 78 sallies for this purpose. In addition, he made 50 flights to defend his territory. Nevertheless, 82 per cent of the bird's daytime was spent perching quietly, once, in the early afternoon, for a half-hour continuously. (This was in sharp contrast to the behavior of the captive white-ear, who in sixteen hours spent fifteen on the wing.) Pearson calculated that his Anna's hummingbird used 10.3 large calories

37

of energy each day if he slept normally, or 7.6 if he became torpid at night. The bird's caloric needs could be supplied by the nectar from the 1,022 blossoms of the single fuchsia bush on which he chiefly depended.

Even on the conservative assumption that a hummingbird consumes half its weight of sugar daily, this is, by human standards, an enormous intake. Greenewalt pointed out that if a man's expenditure of energy, per unit of weight, were as great as a hummingbird's, he would have to devour each day 370 pounds of boiled potatoes or 130 pounds of bread. A normal man eats from two to two and a half pounds of food daily.

A hummingbird has the greatest energy output, gram for gram, of any known warm-blooded animal—apparently of any animals except insects in flight. Why do hummingbirds burn up so much energy? First, because of their very small size. The smaller a body becomes, the more surface it exposes for every gram of its weight and, if the ambient temperature is below that of the body, the more rapidly it loses heat. We humans have a great mass of flesh producing heat for every square inch of skin through which it is dissipated; the hummingbird has a very small mass. Accordingly, to preserve a body temperature considerably higher than ours, the hummingbird must burn much sugar to produce heat. To whir those rapidly beating wings, which apparently generate about as much power on the upstroke as on the downstroke, requires additional energy.

Robert Lasiewski found that at 75 degrees Fahrenheit a hovering Costa's hummingbird consumed oxygen at a rate seven times greater than when it was resting quietly in the dark after having digested its meal. Oxygen consumption at rates varying from 42 to 147 cubic centimeters per gram of body weight per hour has been measured for five species of Californian hummingbirds.

Such studies of hummingbirds' metabolism may seem dryly academic, but they are highly relevant to the question of whether a migrating rubythroat can cross 500 miles of the Gulf of Mexico on a nonstop flight, as field observations suggest it does. Dr. Pearson's early measurements of hummingbirds' energy expenditures in flight indicated that the rubythroat could fly only 385 miles, which, if it started to cross from the mouth of the Mississippi to the tip of the Yucatán Peninsula, would leave it exhausted far from shore. Then it was discovered that, like other birds preparing to migrate, the rubythroat stores up fat to serve as fuel, thereby augmenting its weight by as much as 40 to 50 per cent. This would increase the bird's flying time; but to offset this, it became necessary, in the light of Dr. Greenewalt's observations in a wind tunnel, to halve the original estimate of its speed of 50 miles per hour. Lasiewski's most conservative measurement of the metabolic cost of hummingbird flight suggested that by oxidizing two grams of fat, a male rubythroat could continue to fly for twenty-six hours, which, even at an average speed of 25 miles per hour, would carry it from Louisiana to Yucatán with a good margin of safety. So we can still believe that rubythroats fly between the eastern United States and tropical Mexico by the most direct route.

To be forced always to live at the highest pitch is dangerous, for at times when food is scarce or health impaired, it may not be possible to maintain this pitch, and then life will promptly burn itself out. Hummingbirds often practice small economies in the expenditure of energy by perching or clinging while probing a flower, when a convenient perch is available. But the greatest safeguard that hummingbirds have developed is the capacity to become torpid, with greatly reduced body temperatures, while they sleep, perhaps we could call it "noctivation."

Like other birds, hummingbirds have a higher body temperature than mammals. In a number of species this ranges from about 102° to 108° F. The temperature of a single individual fluctuates a few degrees, according to whether it is quietly resting or active. In normal sleep a hummingbird's temperature may drop four or even eight degrees. In nocturnal torpor its temperature falls much lower than this, almost to that of the surrounding air. Hummingbirds do not noctivate every night, but only when the air is more than about twelve degrees cooler than their normal daytime temperature, or below about 93° F.

Whether or not a hummingbird becomes torpid depends not only upon the air temperature but upon the bird's condition, whether it is well nourished or has deficient reserves, whether it is in good or poor health, and perhaps upon its emotional state. Some hummingbirds in Ruschi's large aviary noctivated almost every night, whereas others rarely did so more than twice a week. Of two hummingbirds of the same kind resting close together, one may become torpid and the other not. By raising their feathers until they bristle, hummingbirds can increase the dissipation of body heat and hasten their descent into torpor—an apparent waste of vital heat that effects an economy.

The noctivating hummingbird cannot fly. Taken in hand, it chirps weakly and moves its limbs feebly. If lifted from its perch, it cannot regain its grip. The duration of torpor is variable. In Ruschi's aviary in southern Brazil, during the cooler season, some hummingbirds noctivated for from eight to fourteen hours, not becoming active until the rising sun had mitigated the early morning chill. In contrast to this, certain North American hummingbirds emerge from torpor before dawn, or in captivity, before lights are turned on, in response to internal rhythm.

The rate of recovery is also variable. Ruschi's hummingbirds could be held in the hand for more than an hour before they became active. Torpid Anna's and Allen's hummingbirds, aroused in the night, could fly more or less competently after ten or fifteen minutes. During arousal, the body temperature rises rapidly, at a rate of a degree or two per minute. The respiration and heartbeats increase correspondingly. Not until they warm up to 86° F or more can they fly.

The energy that a hummingbird saves by becoming torpid depends upon the external temperature. When the air is at 60° F, the noctivating bird may burn only one-fiftieth to one-sixtieth of the fuel that it would need to maintain its body at its usual high temperature. Although the metabolism of a normally resting bird decreases with rising air temperature, because it needs to expend less energy to keep warm, that of a torpid bird increases, as in any cold-blooded animal. At about 95° F the two rates become equal, and doubtless this is the reason why hummingbirds do not noctivate unless the air temperature falls below this level. Incubating and brooding females do not become torpid at night, nor do older nestlings when left exposed. To permit their temperatures to fall would greatly retard the development of embryos and young.

The noctivating animal cannot, without fatal consequences, permit its body fluids and tissues to freeze. In the high Andes, where nocturnal temperatures fall below the freezing point, especially under the dry season's clear skies, and snow, hail, or cold rain by day may curtail the hummingbirds' foraging time, they face special problems. They must noctivate to conserve vital resources, but they cannot do so where radiation into the open sky would result in freezing. Some species, including the Andean hillstar, solve the difficulty by sleeping in caves, abandoned mine shafts, and other protected spots, where even on cold nights the air remains a few degrees above the freezing point. They share these caves with a number of finches, flycatchers, ovenbirds, geese, and even hawks and owls, and in them they also build their nests.

Not long ago ornithologists scoffed at the ancient belief that birds hibernated. Within the past few decades such torpidity has been demonstrated to occur in an increasing number of avian families. The poorwill of western North America may hibernate for months at a time; and swifts of several species become torpid, with greatly reduced body temperatures, when the weather is cold, food is scarce, and they lose weight. African colies, or mousebirds, may also become torpid on cool nights. But perhaps the closest analogy to the noctivation of hummingbirds is provided by the bats, which, like the hummingbirds, include some of the smallest of warm-blooded vertebrates. Active by night, bats of certain species become torpid, with greatly reduced temperatures, in the daytime.

Another aspect of the high intensity at which hummingbirds live is their rapid pulse rate. In the large blue-throated hummingbird this ranges from 36 times per minute during torpidity to 480 while resting quietly at normal temperature and to a high of 1260 times per minute when very active. An excited Anna's Hummingbird breathed 273 times per minute.

Should not animals that live at such high intensity soon burn themselves out? On the contrary, if they escape accidents, hummingbirds have surprisingly long lives. In the Bronx Zoo a greenthroated carib, already grown when acquired, survived ten and one half years of captivity, and a purple-throated carib did so for nine years and eight months. The average life-span of hummingbirds in Ruschi's aviary was about ten years. A female planalto hermit was still alive after fourteen years. Some free-living hummingbirds in the vicinity of Santa Teresa, Brazil, were alive nine years after being banded. A male blue-chested hummingbird who, season after season, sang with unmistakable notes in the same orange tree near our house, was no less than seven years old when he vanished. In general, birds, despite their more rapid metabolism, have a longer potential life-span than mammals of corresponding size, or even much larger ones. Pelicans, eagles, owls, and parrots may, in favorable circumstances, live for more than half a century, and even small passerines, like finches and thrushes, have repeatedly survived in captivity for over twenty years.

Bills and Tongues, Flowers and Insects

To LEARN WHAT HUMMINGBIRDS eat, we must first consider artificial feeding, for it has dispelled certain persistent misconceptions about the diet of hummingbirds, and only with the control possible in an aviary can we learn exactly how much of each kind of food a bird consumes in a day. We should remember, however, that the requirements of a captive bird may differ somewhat from those of the same bird in its natural habitat; it may, for example, be less or more active. And some of the over 300 species of hummingbirds may prefer diets rather different from those of the few kinds that have been studied.

To understand how hummingbirds actually procure their food, we have no substitute for patient observation in their natural habitats. A naturalist interested in the diet of birds pays great attention to the shape of the bill, the organ that most birds, except raptors and parrots, use to gather their food, and which even in those groups has been highly modified for eating it. It is hardly an exaggeration to say that the whole form of a bird, including wings and feet, has been evolved to make the most effective use of its bill; just as our form, our upright posture and all the anatomical peculiarities associated with it, has been modified to make the most effective use of our hands, without which we would starve.

The black, reddish, or yellowish bills of hummingbirds are always
delicately slender; this is one of the most distinctive attributes of the

family. They vary greatly in length and curvature. The eight humming-birds most widespread in temperate North America reveal little of this diversity. Nearly straight, their bills range in length from about nine-sixteenths of an inch in the tiny male calliope hummingbird to about three-quarters of an inch in the female black-chinned (females often have slightly longer bills than males). These North American hummingbirds seem to have the generalized or typical bill of their family, from which those of certain other species have been modified to serve special ends.

The variety of bills among tropical hummingbirds is enormous. In length they range from the four-inch shaft of the sword-billed hummingbird, nearly as long as its body and tail together, to the abbreviated bill of the purple-backed thornbill, only five-sixteenths of an inch long and short-er than its head. In curvature they range from the bills with upturned ends of the fiery-tailed awlbill and mountain avocetbill to the strongly downcurved beak of the white-tipped sicklebill, shaped like a crescent moon. The peculiar form of the bills of other hummingbirds is suggested by such names a saw-billed hermit, hook-billed hermit, and green-fronted lancebill.

Although it is difficult to detect a hummingbird's tongue as it visits flowers, while it perches one sometimes sees it stick out its tongue, a surprisingly long, slender, white organ. Near its base the tongue is a single, flattened tube, with a central constriction that becomes more pro-nounced and soon divides the organ into two narrow tubes lying side by side. About midway along the tongue's length the tubes separate from each other and the wall on the outer side of each splits lengthwise. Each division of the forked tongue now becomes a cartilaginous rod bor-dered by a wide flange of thin membrane, which curls inward, like a narrow strip of paper rolled into tubular form. Toward its end, each flange is fringed; when flattened out, it resembles a feather with the vane on only one side.

The tongue of the hummingbird is uniquely adapted for the extraction of nectar from deep in the cups of flowers.

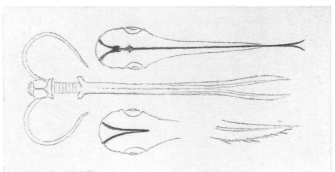

LEFT TOP: Marvelous Spatuletail (*Loddigesia mirabilis*) Peru
LEFT CENTER: Purple-throated Carib (*Eulampis jugularis*) Caribbean Islands
LEFT BOTTOM: Golden-bellied Star-frontlet (*Coeligena bonapartei*) Venezuela, Colombia
RIGHT: Black-hooded Sunbeam (*Agleactis pamela*) Bolivia

This, then, is the apparatus that the hummingbird uses to extract its principal nourishment, nectar, from flowers. The slender bill obviously serves to protect the long, delicate tongue and to aid its entry into the blossom. The bill need not reach all the way to the nectar, because the tongue can stretch beyond it. Just how the tongue operates is not certain, but two possibilities have been suggested. The two very narrow tubes at its end may draw up the sweet liquid by capillarity, or the bird may suck it up, as we drink through a straw. Both actions may be involved, for although capillary attraction can draw liquid into a narrow tube, it cannot make the liquid flow through it. Evidently the hummingbird does not lap up the fluid as a cat drinks milk. The role of the fringes on the edge of each membrane is also doubtful. They may help to sop up the nectar, or they may entangle minute insects that have found their way into the flower.

44

Sketch showing how pollen is deposited on crown of a feeding hummingbird.

Top: Black-throated Mango (*Anthracothorax nigricollis*) Central and northern parts of South America
Center Left: Blue-throated Hummingbird (*Lampornis clemenciae*) Mexico and southwestern U.S.
Center Right: Heloise Hummingbird (*Atthis heloisa*) Mexico

Just as hummingbirds have become, through a long evolution, highly modified to extract nectar from flowers, so flowers have evolved to attract and provide nourishment for hummingbirds, not from altruistic motives, but because these birds serve them well by transferring pollen from plant to plant, with all the evolutionary advantages that cross-fertilization brings. Although hummingbirds can, by one means or another, draw nectar from almost any flower that contains it, those that depend principally upon these birds as pollinators have certain characteristics by which they can be recognized as "hummingbird flowers."

Typical hummingbird flowers are borne in rather open, exposed inflorescences, where the hummingbird can hover in front of them without striking its wings against leaves, twigs, or other members of the inflorescence. They are often trumpet-shaped, or the approach to the nectar is through a tubular part, which may be composed of fused petals   45

Long-billed Starthroat (*Heliomaster longirostris*)
Central America and northwestern South America

Purple-crowned Fairy (*Heliothryx barroti*)
Central America, Colombia, Ecuador.

(gamopetalous) or separate petals fitting closely together (polypetalous). Often the mouth of this tube is surrounded by little or no limb or lip, which might serve as a landing platform for bees or butterflies. Frequently the structure is such as to protect the tender young ovary from injury by the sharp tip of the bird's bill: the stamens may form a sheath around the ovary; grooves may direct the bill to a deposit of nectar somewhat removed from the ovary; or the tube may be so long that only the protruded tongue can reach the ovary. The anthers are so situated that they deposit their pollen upon the visiting bird's crown, throat, or bill; and the stigma that terminates the pistil is placed where it can pick up this pollen. Hummingbird flowers usually secrete copious nectar.

Unlike the fragrant flowers that attract bees and butterflies, or the malodorous minority that draw carrion flies as pollinators, hummingbird flowers are often scentless. It is not to their advantage to be visited by

46

insects that might take their nectar or pollen without paying for it by effecting cross-pollination; and some of their structural features, such as the long, narrow tube and absence of a landing platform, appear to be adaptations to discourage unserviceable visitors. The color of hummingbird flowers is a controversial question to which we shall return; suffice it to say here that hummingbirds visit flowers of all colors.

Considering the great diversity of hummingbirds' bills on the one hand, and the immense variety of sizes and shapes of flowers that conform to the broad hummingbird pattern on the other hand, we should expect certain hummingbirds to prefer certain flowers rather than to visit all indiscriminately. Although apparently no example of the restriction of a species of hummingbird to flowers of a single species, genus, or even family exists, certain preferences are clearly evident. As I write, I can look through my open window at a poró tree, beneath which is a cluster of stachytarpheta shrubs. The poró, a species of the large leguminous genus *Erythrina*, has flowers three and a half inches long, composed largely of a robust papillonaceous standard folded into a long, narrow, sword-shaped tube that tightly encloses all the other floral parts except the thick, fleshy calyx that forms a collar around its base. The stachytarpheta, a member of the verbena family, has delicate little florets with a narrow tube half an inch long.

At intervals through the day, a long-billed starthroat, whose straight bill is one and one-fourth inches long, visits the red flowers of the poró tree that he claims as his own. Less frequently, a female violet-headed hummingbird, a much smaller species with a bill only half an inch long, makes the rounds of the violet stachytarpheta florets, consistently ignoring the poró, whose nectar is not readily accessible to her. Similarly, the starthroat never visits the stachytarpheta nor chases the little violet-head, as he does every larger hummer that he sees near his poró tree.

Although many exceptions occur, in general, large hummingbirds prefer large flowers, while small hummingbirds are content to visit small ones, including those as tiny as the florets of a typical composite. One reason why large hummers tend to neglect small flowers may be that they do not yield enough nectar to restore the energy spent in visiting them. One can roughly estimate the amount of nectar a flower yields by the time a hummingbird devotes to it. A hummingbird's visit to a small floret is almost instantaneous, and many such flowers are sucked dry in a few seconds. A large flower may entertain the hummingbird for several seconds.

Long-tailed Hermit (*Phaethornis superciliosus*)
Northern South America.

Mountain Avocetbill (*Opisthoprora euryptera*)
Colombia, Ecuador.

White-tipped Sicklebill (*Eutoxeres aquila*)
Colombia, Ecuador.

Bills of unusual size or shape are adapted to flowers of unusual size or shape. The enormous bill of the sword-billed hummingbird enables it to exploit the huge, pendent bells of the arborescent daturas of the Andes and perhaps other gigantic flowers. The white-tipped sicklebill is closely associated with certain wild plantains, or heliconias, whose tubular, yellow flowers, embraced by thick, furry, dull red bracts in a long, flat, dangling inflorescence, have a curvature like that of the bird's bill. While probing these flowers, the sicklebill prefers to cling beside them with its exceptionally stout feet rather than to hover.

Access to the nectar of the scarlet passionflower is guarded by a narrow collar that makes these six-inch-wide blossoms almost the special preserve of the long-billed long-tailed hermit, at least in this valley. On long, nearly leafless shoots, these flamboyant flowers are displayed near the ground, in the woodland shade where the hermit dwells, while the passionflower vine scrambles high in the trees to spread its three-lobed leaves in the sunshine. Despite some specialization, an attractive flower may be visited by many kinds of hummingbirds.

Although hummingbirds and their flowers have evolved simultaneously and become reciprocally adapted to their mutual advantage, this relationship has in some cases been violated, as happens too often in the living world. The purple-crowned fairy, outstanding in grace even in a graceful family, is, I regret to relate, an incorrigible thief. With a short and exceptionally sharp bill, it habitually pierces the bases of flowers of the most diverse kinds, simply by pressing against them while hovering, and extracts the nectar through the perforation, without ever transferring a grain of pollen. It can even plunder in this fashion the well-enclosed flowers of the poro, when the long-billed starthroat who claims them

48

Sword-billed Hummingbird (*Ensifera ensifera*)
Northern South America.

Purple-backed Thornbill (*Ramphomicron microrhynchum*)
Northern South America.

is not looking. This irregular method of procuring nectar gives the fairy an unusually wide choice of flowers.

Some hummingbirds that usually take nectar in the "legitimate" manner occasionally puncture long corolla tubes. They regularly treat in this way the long, golden trumpets of the native guayacán and the great, red flowers of the flame-of-the-forest tree, introduced from Africa. A genus of honeycreepers, the flower-piercers or diglossas, have bills highly specialized for extracting nectar through perforations in the bases of tubular corollas. And, as is well known, bees frequently bite holes in corolla tubes or spurs to suck up nectar that they cannot otherwise reach.

Often a hummingbird claims possession of a patch of flowers, part of a garden, a profusely blossoming shrub, or perhaps certain branches of a big flowering tree, thereby establishing a "feeding territory." By threatening darts, it tries to chase away all intruders, especially hummingbirds of its own or different species, regardless of sex, sometimes nectar-drinking songbirds such as bananaquits, and even large bees and butterflies. If an invading hummingbird resists, the two may grapple and fall to the ground, fighting fiercely. In the tropics, where resident birds are, on the whole, milder-tempered than the migratory species of higher latitudes, I have rarely seen such stubborn conflicts as others have described in the North; here, the intruder is usually chased away without physical contact. These territories are likely to break down if the flowers are highly attractive and hummingbirds of many kinds swarm to them; the cost of defense becomes too great. In any case, the temporary territory is abandoned when the defended plants cease blooming or the migratory hummingbird resumes its journey.

Much has been written about the color preferences of hummingbirds, a subject perennially attractive to experimenters, who offer them syrup colored with different food dyes, or perhaps colorless syrup in tubes surrounded by artificial corollas of various hues. Others have carefully listed the species and colors of all the flowers that hummingbirds are known to visit.

49

It appears to be true that at least a small majority of hummingbird flowers are some shade of red, and in certain regions this majority may be large. Red is the color most likely to attract attention amid nature's greenery, not only that of ourselves, but also that of birds, whose color vision seems not to differ much from ours. Likewise, red is less attractive to bees, whose greatest sensitivity to color lies toward the violet end of the spectrum and beyond, and which might steal nectar without pollinating flowers adapted to hummingbird pollination. Many North American hummingbird flowers have evolved from bee flowers, with a shift from blue or violet to red, along with structural changes.

Red, as those responsible for traffic control are well aware, is the color most likely to arrest our attention; but this does not mean that we prefer red to blue or yellow or some other color. The same seems to be true of hummingbirds. Like a thrifty housewife, they are more interested in the contents of the package than the wrapping, however eye-catching the latter may be. They can detect small differences in the concentration of sugar solutions and prefer the sweeter ones; when the syrup contains less than one part of sugar to eight parts of water, they disdain it. They explore their environment, and when they discover a rich source of nectar, honey, or sugar, they exploit it, whatever its color or that of its container, and even if it is colorless.

Like ourselves, hummingbirds form associations and habits. If for some time they have been drinking from a red flower or feeder, they continue to expect food where they see this color. Likewise, they associate food with a certain position, which they persist in visiting even when the color of the syrup placed in that spot has been changed; the attraction of the position may outweigh that of the color. The persistence of habit was neatly demonstrated by Helmuth Wagner in Mexico. He found that when the free hummingbirds in the neighborhood were getting most of their nectar from purple flowers, they came most often to his purple flasks; at another season, when blue flowers were blooming profusely, they drank freely from his blue feeders and neglected the purple ones.

Because of the power of association, it can be advantageous to the plants that depend upon hummingbirds for pollination, as well as to the birds themselves, to have all their flowers a single color. This would be especially true in a region where the hummingbirds are migratory and all have bills of nearly the same length and shape, so that the flower suitable for one would be suitable for all. Then, wherever it might be,

Most hummingbirds supplement their diet of nectar with insects either caught while they are sitting on flowers or in flight.

White-necked Jacobin (*Florisuga mellivora*) Central America and northern South America

the traveling hummingbird would look for a red flower to assuage its thirst, just as we might look for a red sign when we wish to find an exit. As Karen and Verne Grant have shown, in the western United States, where hummingbirds are usually migratory, most of their flowers are red. The advantage of having all hummingbird flowers of one color, hence the strength of the evolutionary forces effecting this convergence, would be less in a tropical region where, because of differences in bills, not all hummingbird flowers are readily available to all hummingbirds, and where, moreover, the more stationary birds would learn to recognize their flowers specifically, for which differences in color, rather than uniformity, might be helpful.

The insects that hummingbirds need to provide protein and round out their diet are captured in various ways. Some naturalists have supposed that most are obtained from inside flowers, and that these birds visit the flowers primarily for insects rather than for nectar. This seems a most unsatisfactory way of gathering insects. Many flowers that hummingbirds visit have narrow tubes, or are otherwise so constructed that the birds could not see what they contain and would have to grope blindly for insects. And how would they remove them? Hardly, as some have supposed, by sticking to their tongues; Walter Scheithauer could

51

not make an insect adhere to a hummingbird's tongue by pressing it there. The forked tongue does not appear able to function as a pincers for seizing insects, and the tubes are so narrow that they would be clogged by all but the minutest of them. Hummingbirds have better ways of catching insects.

One often sees a hummingbird hovering with its bill close to the bark of a tree, a twig, a green leaf, the wall of a house, or the outside of a flower. Perhaps it is searching for cobweb for its nest, but often it is hunting the tiny insects and spiders that lurk in such places. Some hummingbirds become adept at removing insects caught in spiders' webs, and the spider itself if of small size, without themselves becoming ensnared.

Many insects are captured in flight, by darting out from an exposed perch or by dashing into the midst of a swarm of hovering gnats. When it finds such good hunting, the bird darts this way and that, often going only a few inches in each direction, abruptly changing its course with great frequency, and tracing a most intricate trajectory. Movement is so swift, the prey so small and quickly swallowed, that it is hardly possible to see whether anything is captured, but apparently the hummingbird is eating well. Hummingbirds rarely, if ever, dismember their prey, as many other insectivorous birds do; they take only those minute enough to be swallowed.

As an instrument for catching insects, the hummingbird's long, thin bill seems greatly inferior to the broad, flat bill of a flycatcher or swallow or the capacious mouth of a swift or goatsucker. Moreover, it lacks the rictal bristles around the mouth that are believed to help deflect flying insects into it. The hummingbird compensates for the narrowness of its bill by its superb control of flight. It pursues the insects until it catches them.

When a hummingbird catches an insect in flight, its forward movement may force the tiny creature so far back into its mouth that it is readily swallowed. When it picks up a stationary insect in the tip of its long bill, it faces a problem—how to move the insect far enough back to be swallowed. It is easy to see how another long-billed bird, the toucan, solves this problem. It gives its head an upward jerk and at the critical moment opens its great colorful beak, thereby tossing the berry or insect back into its throat. Scheithauer saw his captive hummingbirds proceed in much the same fashion, with the difference that instead of only jerking up the head, they swung the whole body upward while in flight.

Dependence upon insects and the method of catching them vary with the species of hummingbird and its environment. The white-necked Jacobin prefers to dart about erratically in the midst of a swarm of gnats, snatching them up right and left. The long, curved bills of the hermits seem inappropriate for this sort of work; instead of catching insects in the air, they hover amid the undergrowth of tropical woodland, gleaning insects and spiders mostly from the undersides of leaves. When flowers are scarce at the height of a tropical dry season, or in the cooler periods at high altitudes or high latitudes, hummingbirds depend more upon insects than when there is no lack of nectar.

The little pits that sapsuckers freely drill in the bark of living trees serve hummingbirds as well as the industrious woodpeckers who make them. Of the twenty kinds of birds that William Foster and James Tate found visiting sapsucker pits in Michigan, ruby-throated hummingbirds came most frequently—more often than the yellow-bellied sapsuckers themselves. They not only imbibed the sugary sap but caught many of the smaller insects that were also attracted to it. At the northern limit of their breeding range in Saskatchewan, Canada, ruby-throated hummingbirds arrive in the spring a month or more before plants flower freely. In the interval, the borings of sapsuckers help sustain them. In western North America at least three other hummingbird species profit by sapsuckers' work; but in tropical America, apart from a few migrants, sap-sucking woodpeckers are unknown. In addition to sap from trees, hummingbirds occasionally sip the juices of sweet, ripe fruits.

In a family so large and varied as the hummingbirds, idiosyncracies are to be expected. Although most hummingbirds never walk even two inches, in Bolivia, nearly 15,000 feet above sea level, François Vuilleumier watched an olivaceous thornbill walking over the densely matted grass cushions of a meadow and picking up insects, with an occasional dart into the air to seize one in flight. Similar terrestrial foraging, so unexpected in hummingbirds, has been reported also of the bearded helmetcrest and a few related species of the high Andes. Equally foreign to our usual experience with hummingbirds is the practice of picking up minute grains of sand, as Nicholaas Verbeek saw Anna's hummingbirds do repeatedly in California and has been reported of a few other species. Evidently the purpose of this behavior is to obtain calcium for forming eggshells, or to replace calcium that was borrowed from the skeleton when the eggs were laid.

Daily Activities and Temperament

HUMMINGBIRDS BATHE FREQUENTLY. Often I have watched one fly down to a still woodland pool, half immerse itself in the limpid water, then without pausing rise to an overhanging twig, to shake out the water and arrange its plumage. As befits so aerial a creature, it may bathe at greater heights, skimming over the broad surface of a banana leaf, or some other giant leaf laden with raindrops or dew, or else fluttering amid dripping foliage. Sometimes hummingbirds press against a saturated cushion of green moss on a tree trunk until their feathers are wet. Or they may bathe by spreading their plumage so that raindrops can penetrate to the skin.

Standing on a dam in a deep, flowery ravine high in the Costa Rican mountains, I passed hours enjoying the hummingbirds who came to bathe in the clear, cold water, often so near my feet that I could have touched them. In two hours one bright morning, twenty-eight baths were taken by male and female hummingbirds of four species, some of whom may have repeated. Clinging to the lip of the dam, or to a mossy rock at the brink of the high waterfall below it, each pressed body and head down into the shallow, smoothly flowing water while, with spread, vibrating wings, it splashed shining drops over its glittering plumage.

Aviculturists find immense enjoyment watching their hummingbirds bathe in the most various ways. Given a vessel with water only half

54

Hummingbirds can bathe in different ways, taking advantage of water wherever it is found.

LEFT: Rufous-tailed Hummingbird (*Amazilia tzacatl*) Colombia, Venezuela, Ecuador

RIGHT: Fork-tailed Woodnymph (*Thalurania furcata*) Central and South America

an inch deep, some sit in it and splash like songbirds. A sword-billed hummingbird prostrated itself in the dish, completely submerging its long bill. A violet-bellied hummingbird immersed only its underparts, and with beating wings sailed around in circles, like a tiny flying boat.

While Emerson Stoner watered his garden in California, a female Anna's hummingbird often came to flit through the spray from his hose. One day she discovered that she could ride the stream, a solid jet of water about three-quarters of an inch thick. Flying up at right angles, she alighted on the jet, as though it were a branch, and permitted it to carry her forward. Over and over she did this, apparently enjoying the stunt. She seemed to be playing rather than bathing.

Because they so often dash after each other in hot pursuit, hummingbirds have acquired a reputation for pugnacity, which perhaps they do not deserve. Since at times they seem to play, and to enjoy flight for its own sake, may not their wild chases be often undertaken in a sportive rather than a hostile spirit? At least, so it has appeared to me as well as to other watchers of hummingbirds. It is true that they never fly in flocks and that the nesting female is nearly always alone. But at their courtship assemblies, a number of males, who are evidently rivals, sing day after day within sight and hearing of their neighbors, a situation that could not persist if they were fiercely hostile to each other. In an aviary hummingbirds thrive better, and seem more cheerful, in company with others rather than alone. They never preen mutually or cuddle together for warmth, as certain other cage birds do, but they appear

LEFT: Rivoli's Hummingbird (*Eugenes fulgens*) S.W. United States, Mexico, Central America

Scaly-breasted Hummingbird (*Phaeochroa cuvierii*) Central America, Colombia

to need the stimulus of battles, earnest or playful, with companions as agile on the wing as themselves. The swift pursuits, the dodges and maneuvers, add zest to their lives and help keep them in good condition.

No bird can preen its own head or throat, and the longer its bill, the greater the extent of plumage that cannot be reached by it. Toucans and ibises solve the difficulty by preening each other's heads and necks, a method employed by many highly social birds. After the nestling stage, unsocial hummingbirds have not been seen to groom each other. They can attend to their heads only by scratching, which they do by dropping a wing and raising the foot on the same side over it, in the "indirect" head-scratching usually followed by passerine birds.

Possibly because their movements are so swift that they can elude threats which would be disastrous to other birds, hummingbirds are exceptionally bold. With their fearlessness goes an unusual degree of curiosity. Sometimes while advancing laboriously through the tangled vegetation of warm tropical lowlands, I have been approached by a brown hermit, often a band-tailed barbthroat, who for the better part of a minute has hovered all around me, so close that the breeze from its invisible wings has fanned my heated face and I might have reached out and touched it—or at least the spot where it hung motionless while inspecting me. Its curiosity satisfied, with a little chirp it would shoot away through the dense growth where I could not follow. Occasionally, returning the confidence, a perching hermit has permitted me to bend over and scrutinize it no less closely. I suspect that hummingbirds are nearsighted. They need to be, in order to focus sharply upon the tiny insects that they catch in flight hardly an inch from their eyes.

Hummingbirds show their curiosity in other ways. Not long ago, I noticed a little hermit inspecting the red label on a broom handle on the porch. By exploring their surroundings, especially objects whose color stands out from the prevailing greens and browns, they discover new sources of food. Inquisitiveness helps them survive.

Curiosity reveals a modicum of intelligence, or capacity to learn about the environment and adapt to altered situations. Although the brains in such diminutive bodies are necessarily small, hummingbirds are no more stupid than many larger birds. They show no insect-like insensitivity to danger; at their nests they tend to be as wary as many of the passerine birds of the same region, and I have commonly been obliged to use the same precautions when studying them. If they blunder into a room, some hover close to the ceiling, ignoring open windows and doors below them, utterly confused when, for the first time in their lives, they find an impassable barrier overhead—just as many songbirds do in similar circumstances. I have seen other hummingbirds, however, remain calm and explore the walls, glass windows, and screens of a room until they found a path to freedom.

One of the most intelligent acts that I have found recorded of a hummingbird was related by W. L. Dawson and repeated in Bent's life histories. When a black-chinned hummingbird was somehow trapped in a porch by a wall of chicken-wire netting with meshes an inch and a half wide, it flew slowly along the screen, seeking a broader exit. Since none was found, it darted through a mesh. This act would have wrecked its wings if the bird had not folded them at the precise moment of passing through. The maneuver was accomplished too quickly for the human eye to follow details; but a momentary break in the sound of the beating wings revealed that it had furled them. Probably hummingbirds have few occasions to fly through gaps so narrow that they must reduce their spread, and this was an original adaptation to a novel situation.

Although mutual aid has been recorded of a number of more social birds, who may feed each other's young and attend ailing companions, one hardly expects it of unsocial hummingbirds. When a female calliope hummingbird dashed against a window in Montana and fell, stunned and motionless, to the ground, a male of her kind immediately flew up and hovered over her. Seizing her bill in his, he rose directly upward and lifted her about three feet, before she slipped from his grasp and fell. Twice more he tried to carry her off, always with the same result. Then he flew away, leaving her lying motionless. A few minutes later, the stunned female recovered in human hands. What was the male's motive in trying to bear away the injured female?

In the evening twilight, after other diurnal birds have gone to rest, hummingbirds fly actively from flower to flower, filling their stomachs with nectar to sustain them through the night, which in the tropics is always long and, at high altitudes, often very cold. Then they dart away, colorless little figures in the dusk, to sleeping places that are rarely found. The few times that I have discovered them on their roosts, they were sleeping with neck retracted, head exposed, and bill pointed forward with a more or less upward tilt—not with head turned back and buried in the shoulder feathers in the usual manner of birds. This is the way others have found them roosting. On the nest, too, the incubating or brooding mother sleeps with her head forward and exposed.

Although most small birds prefer to sleep well-screened by foliage, if not in dormitary nests, some hummingbirds are careless of concealment. This is the way of the long-billed starthroat, which I have repeatedly found roosting on a thin twig at the very top of a tall, dying guava tree on a hilltop, as conspicuous against the sky as such a small bird can be. The starthroat often builds its nest in a situation hardly less exposed; apparently it has few aerial enemies.

These birds, and also scaly-breasted hummingbirds that I have watched settle down for the night, behave most curiously. After alighting on their roost, they twitch their head rapidly from side to side, continuing these apparently aimless movements sometimes for only a few minutes, sometimes for as long as a quarter of an hour. Gradually the head movements decrease in amplitude, until finally the bird becomes motionless, its head still exposed.

Directing a flashlight beam upon a starthroat resting, if not sleeping, on its treetop, I was surprised by the bright reflection from its tiny eyes. This gleam suggested that the hummingbird might have fairly good night vision. Nevertheless, unless disturbed or migrating, hummingbirds are not known to be active in the dark.

Courtship, Voice, and Other Sounds

THE MORE TIME THAT BIRDS can take to find nuptial partners, the less obtrusively they do it. Many constantly mated birds of mild climates pair long before they breed, in a manner so obscure that it escapes those who watch them closely. Among migratory birds that pair only for the breeding season, the urgency to find a partner is greater, and the male, after acquiring a territory, sings profusely until he attracts a female. Since the sexes come together only long enough to fertilize the female's developing eggs, she must be able to find a suitable male promptly, before the critical period passes. Accordingly, the males of such birds have developed some of the most spectacular and efficient means of self-advertisement. Of all the familes of birds in which the association of the sexes is, for all or most species, a transitory affair, hummingbirds are the largest. Their methods of attracting the other sex are among the most varied and engaging of all.

Among animals in general, the sexes are brought together by visual, auditory, and olfactory signals. The latter are apparently absent in birds, whose sense of smell is poorly developed. Those that dwell in open country can depend largely upon visual advertisement; but amid the heavy tropical vegetation where many hummingbirds live, visual signals are effective only at close range. The males of many tropical hummingbirds announce their presence by their voices. And since a hummingbird's

Elliot's Hummingbird (*Atthis ellioti*) Central America, male and female

voice is too weak to carry far, it overcomes this deficiency by cooperating with other hummingbirds. In many species, a number of males gather in a certain locality to form a courtship or singing assembly. Such an assembly is a fairly permanent institution, persisting in the same spot for years, often until a change in the habitat forces its abandonment. This adds to the advantage of calling together that of having a traditional locality where the females learn they will find a choice of males. Between these concentrations of singing male hummingbirds may be long distances in which none is found.

The number of hummingbirds in an assembly ranges from 2 or 3 to, rarely, 100 or more, as was reported of the long-tailed hermit in Guyana by T. A. W. Davis. The assemblies of hermits of all species are usually situated amid rather dense undergrowth of primary forest or taller second growth. Each participant rests upon a slender twig, often less than a yard above the ground, where his brownish body blends so well with the brown fallen leaves that he would be difficult to detect if he did not so constantly wag his white-tipped tail up and down while he sings.

More brilliant hummingbirds, such as the violet-headed, blue-throated goldentail, and green violet-ear, perform high up in the trees. Or in some species, such as the white-eared hummingbird, the singing male may alternate between high and low stations. Whatever the site, each participant has his own particular perch, or several neighboring perches, where he is to be found day after day throughout a long season. Here he is within hearing, if not also within sight, of one or more other singing males, although in a large assembly the more widely separated members may be out of contact with each other. From time to time, one male invades another's post, giving rise to a spirited chase. Soon, however, both are back at their usual stations, feathers unruffled, singing as tirelessly as ever.

The season when these assemblies are active varies from species to species, even in the same region, and are a good indication of when each nests. Here in southern Costa Rica, violet-headed hummingbirds and blue-throated goldentails sing chiefly in the dry season and fall silent when the rains become heavy. Band-tailed barbthroats hardly begin to sing until showers have refreshed the forest, continue through the early rainy months, but cease long before the wet season ends. The little hermit performs through most of the year, except at the height of the dry seasons, when flowers are scarce, and in the months of the heaviest deluges.

The daily period of song also differs from species to species. Rufous-tailed hummingbirds start to sing in the dim light of dawn and stop for the day soon after sunrise. The blue-chested hummingbirds perform in the morning and again in the late afternoon; only in periods of greatest zeal do they continue throughout the day. Some of the hermits and the green violet-ears sing tirelessly all day long, with such intensity that they appear to be highly efficient machines for transmuting nectar into squeaks. Some of these all-day singers interrupt their recitals only long enough to wet their throats with nectar from the nearest flowers and to chase trespassers. They spend about as much of the day at their singing stations as an incubating female of their kind does on her eggs.

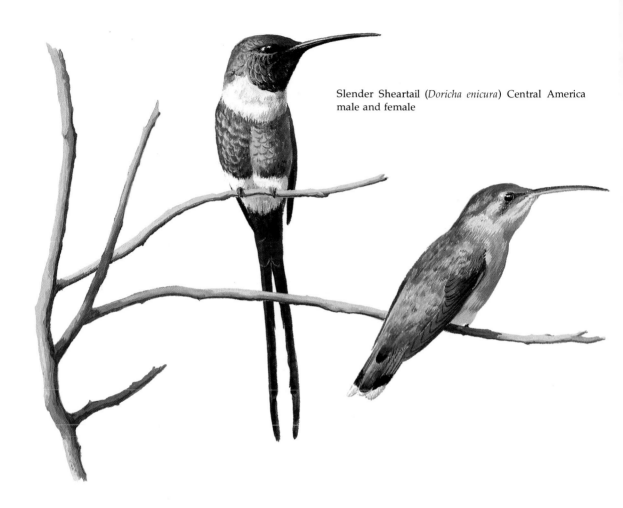

Slender Sheartail (*Doricha enicura*) Central America male and female

A group of male birds gathered together in one spot to attract females by collective advertisement is often called a lek. In a typical lek, such as that of ruffs or manakins, a visiting female freely chooses one of the competing males; they go through a more or less elaborate nuptial ceremony on his display station; and the mating is consummated then and there. With the more mobile hummingbirds the course of events appears to be different. Various naturalists have, in aggregate, spent a great many hours watching their courtship assemblies without witnessing coition. Often, however, we see one hummingbird visit a male at his station, and before we can make sure of the newcomer's sex, the two streak away together, to be promptly lost from view amid the surrounding vegetation. The full courtship ceremony seems usually, if not always, to be performed at a distance from the assembly.

In contrast to the far-flung aerobatics of certain hummingbirds of more open country, these woodland dwellers perform on a much more modest scale, as the air space available for their displays may be limited. None the less, some give a charming performance. Bending up his head and tail until he resembles a miniature boat with high-peaked prow and stern, floating on an invisible fluid above and slightly in front of a female perching low, the little hermit darts back and forth for a foot or less, pivots around in the air, and dips toward his spectator, while his invisible wings buzz more loudly than in ordinary flight. This display may continue for ten minutes or more, during which the silent female never ceases to follow every movement of the floating bird with her head. Once, at a distance from an assembly, I saw the wooer try twice to mount the one above whom he had performed, but each time she eluded his advances. A related hummingbird, the rufous hermit of South America, sticks out his long, white tongue toward the female, who warbles sweetly while watching him display before her.

In more open country on the high plateau of Mexico, Helmuth Wagner has witnessed, and recorded in detailed sketches, the courtship flight that often ensues when a female enters a male's territory. Flying closely side by side, the two trace intricate courses through the air, with many

Blue-throated Star-frontlet (*Coeligena helianthea*) Colombia, Venezuela

The aerial courtship of hummingbirds is often intricate.

The courtship flight varies from species to species, and even within the same species there are usually several variations on the same theme.

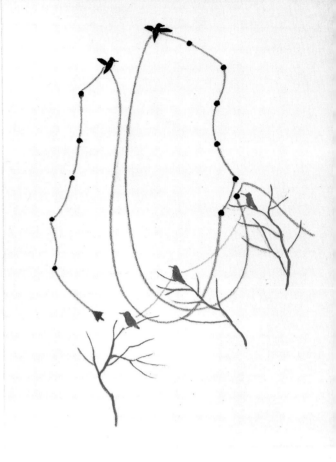

Broad-tailed Hummingbird
(*Selasphorus platycercus*) Western U.S., Mexico, Guatemala

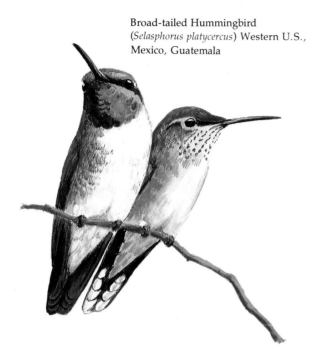

loops or zigzags, at intervals pausing to hover face to face or wing to wing. But always they fly beyond view before the consummation of their aerial courtship.

Although the advertisement display of some hummingbirds consists of little more than monotonous calling from a perch, others, including the green violet-ear and the wine-throated hummingbird, vary their procedure by singing in flight, either passing from one tree to another or looping around to return to their starting point. Thus we can trace the transition from species in which the male tries to lure the female by voice alone, through those in which visual is combined with vocal display, to those in which the display is primarily visual. Such sounds as accompany the most spectacular visual displays are made by air passing through attenuated or otherwise modified wing or tail feathers, or perhaps by striking their thickened shafts together.

Of the eight hummingbirds that breed north of the southern fringe of the United States, only one, the Anna's hummingbird, has a reputation for singing, and its song evidently corresponds to the juvenile song rather than the advertising song of tropical hummingbirds. All, including the

64

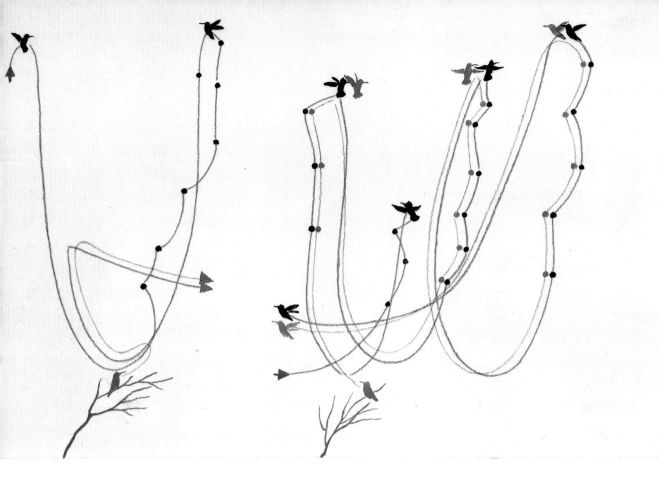

Anna's, draw attention to themselves by their sonorous flight and spectacular aerial displays. Since in fairly open country they can make themselves so conspicuous, they have no need to cooperate in courtship assemblies to attract the females. Except for three broad-tailed hummingbirds that displayed only a few yards apart, as recently reported by David Barash, the hummingbirds of temperate North America appear always to have been watched displaying alone.

These eight hummingbirds are the ruby-throated, black-chinned, Costa's, Anna's, broad-tailed, rufous, Allen's, and calliope. The displays of all consist in looping back and forth in spectacular dives, followed by ascents that make the trajectory symmetrical about its lowest point. The courses followed by the different species differ chiefly in height and openness; they range from a U that may be well over 100 feet high to a much lower, broader, more open arc. The latter is the course of the rubythroat; while some of the western species, including the broad-tailed, Allen's, Costa's, and Anna's, trace the towering U's.

The last-mentioned bird adds a refinement absent from the performances of the others. While ascending to the point from which he will dive, the male Anna's keeps his eyes upon the object of his display, which may be a female perching low, some other bird, or even a man. Then he plunges downward almost vertically in a power dive that achieves tremendous speed and levels off so as to pass over the object headed straight into the sun, which, shining full upon his iridescent gorget, makes it glow with electric brilliance. At the moment of shooting over the display object, he makes an explosive noise with his tail.

In Central America these high, U-shaped flights are made by the broad-tailed hummingbird in alpine meadows and on flowery open slopes at the southern limit of its range, by the rose-throated hummingbird of the loftiest Costa Rican mountaintops, and perhaps by other species of *Selasphorus*. Above the treeline in Peru, Jean Dorst watched Andean hill-stars and sparkling hummingbirds trace high, inverted U's and vertical-loops, the later singing at the flat top of their trajectory. But, as far as I know, no equally extended flight displays have been reported from tropical forests and the clearings among them.

The final stages of the Andean hillstar's courtship take place in the female's nesting territory. Probably to make him feel more at ease there, she feeds him repeatedly, as though he were a fledgling, and this leads to coition. The feeding of an adult male by a female is not otherwise known among hummingbirds and is most exceptional in the whole avian class, in which nuptial feeding is usually done by the male to the female. Although aerial coition has been reported in hummingbirds, this may have been a misinterpretation of a grappling conflict; although rarely witnessed, coition seems usually to occur while the female perches. Only among swifts is aerial coition well authenticated, and it is by no means invariable, for the male may also mount his mate in their nest space.

The more breathtaking and dashing the male hummingbird's display, the more ornate, the more different from the female, he becomes. He tends to develop a dazzling, expansible gorget that he can flash in the face of the female as he speeds toward her. Hummingbirds with singing assemblies show less pronounced sexual differences in appearance; often the sexes are nearly alike. These, however, are only trends in the develop-ment of hummingbirds' plumage, to which exceptions are known, and more will doubtless be discovered.

I have deliberately used the word "song" for the utterances that hum-mingbirds repeat in their courtship assemblies to attract females because

66

functionally they correspond to the usually more brilliant vocal outpourings of songbirds. Many of these songs, however, consist of no more than one or two squeaky, harsh, or metallic notes, repeated over and over with the most tiresome monotony, often hundreds of times with hardly a pause. Yet there are tremendous differences in the tone and complexity of the utterances that one hears in these assemblies, and some are much more melodious than others.

Without being a brilliant songster, the little hermit often achieves a pleasant lilt and cadence. The band-tailed barbthroat's elaborate song, heard in the dim solitude of the lowest level of tropical forests, sounds melancholy, as though the hermit yearned for a mate or perhaps for the sunlight. Admirers of the wedge-tailed saberwing of Mexico have dubbed it the "singing hummingbird" and the "nightingale hummingbird." I have never heard this melodious bird, but I wonder whether its song surpasses that of the exquisite little gem of the Guatemalan mountains, the wine-throated hummingbird, whose sweetly varied outpouring continues for the better part of a minute. If it were only a little more forceful, it might win for its author a place among the world's renowned songsters.

If an observer compares the songs heard in different courtship assemblies of the same species in the same locality, he notices a curious fact. The birds in the same assembly all sing very much alike, but their songs may differ from those that prevail in another assembly not half a mile away, sometimes so strikingly that until he has examined the singers carefully through field glasses, he may suspect that they belong to different species. This, which I first noticed many years ago among white-eared hummingbirds in the Guatemalan mountains, has since been found true of other species, and has been substantiated by sound recordings, notably in the little hermit. These differences can hardly be hereditary, for the different song groups are not reproductively isolated. The hummingbirds learn their songs; when a young bird joins a courtship assembly, which may have been established for many years, he evidently copies the song pattern prevailing there.

Further evidence that hummingbirds learn their songs was provided by a blue-chested hummingbird who, year after year, performed in an orange tree near our house. Close by the assembly of blue-chested hummingbirds to which he belonged was one of rufous-tailed hummingbirds, and he had somehow picked up the song of this related species, very different from that of his own kind. Once having acquired this alien utterance, he never relinquished it; but he repeated it in the late afternoon as well as at dawn, as blue-chests do but rufous-tails do not.

In addition to their loud, advertising song, hummingbirds have another, quite different one. Sometimes you will see a male hump his back, depress his neck, tilt up his bill, and swell out his throat, although his mouth remains closed. The vibrations of his throat feathers suggest that he is singing, but unless you are near and all is quiet, you are not likely to detect the weak notes that he pours forth continuously for many seconds, as when we hum a tune to ourselves. I have heard young males fed by their mothers sing in this fashion, notably among the scaly-breasted hummingbirds and the purple-throated mountain-gems. Adult males in singing assemblies frequently interrupt their louder, open-mouthed singing to swell out their throats and sing sotto voce; and one may hear such subdued vocalization at other times when hummingbirds seem well-fed, idle, and happy. Hummingbirds are most persistent songsters, and, moreover, both sexes express their emotions with a variety of chirps, squeaks, and twitters.

These scarcely audible songs of hummingbirds evidently correspond to the earliest songs of songbirds, which are often sweet, long-continued, rambling melodies, quite different from the definitive songs that some of these birds will soon develop. Sometimes, as in certain wrens, these juvenile songs are more delightful than the adult songs; but they do not suffice for specific recognition, and if retained, they would not serve an important function of song.

The transition from the diffuse, low, juvenile songs of hummingbirds to the louder, mostly shorter, stereotyped songs of adult hummingbirds in courtship assemblies reminds us strongly of the course of song development in songbirds, some of which learn their songs from older birds, while others inherit them. And it is quite different from the development of voice in the more songful nonpasserines, such as jacamars, and even in "lower" passerines, such as woodcreepers and cotingas. While still in the nest, some of these birds already repeat songs that hardly differ from those of adults except in volume and appear to be innate rather than learned.

Consideration of the course of voice development in hummingbirds, along with other aspects of their lives, raises the suspicion that they might, after all, be songbirds, or at least derived from an early oscine stock, with reduction of their vocal organs to conform to the size of their bodies.

Where wing or tail feathers are modified for making sounds, as in a number of the northernmost hummingbirds, voice loses much of its importance. The word "hummingbird" seems to have been first applied to the rubythroat by English colonists on the eastern seaboard of North America. Thus the name by which we know the family was first bestowed upon a species with exceptionally sonorous flight. If English-speaking people had first become familiar with living hummingbirds in the tropics, where many fly more silently, we would probably have a different name for them. The designations given to these birds in the Latin American countries where they abound seldom refer to their wing sounds. In Central America their vulgar name is *gorrión*, which in Spain means sparrow! *Chupaflor* (flower-sucker) and *picaflor* (flower-pecker) are names given to hummingbirds in other Spanish-speaking countries. But the Brazilians have hit upon the most apt and poetic designation. They call the hummingbird *beija-flôr,* which in Portugese means "kiss-flower."

Nesting

IN NEARLY ALL OF the few species of hummingbirds that have been somewhat adequately studied, the female associates with a male only long enough to fertilize her eggs. As a rule, she builds her nest not only out of sight and hearing of courting males but at a good distance from other females. Rarely does one find two hummingbirds nesting close together. Above a brook in the midst of tropical forest I once, to my great surprise, discovered two violet-headed hummingbirds' nests only four feet apart, one with feathered nestlings and the other with eggs that a second female was incubating. In another year I found two little hermits incubating only twelve feet apart and consistently ignoring each other.

Truly colonial nesting occurs in the Chimborazo hillstars that live between 13,000 and 15,000 feet on shapely Volcán Cotopaxi in Ecuador, just below the great ice cap, where snow, hail, fierce gales, and freezing nocturnal temperatures are frequent. To rear their young, these hill stars must seek the protection of shallow caves in the walls of deep ravines. In one such cave Corley Smith discovered five occupied nests within a radius of seven feet—apparently the greatest concentration of hummingbirds' nests on record. He found the males and females segregated in different ravines, probably an arrangement to save more nearby food for the females and their young. Rufous hummingbirds sometimes build a dozen or more nests in a small area, the closest only a few yards apart.

A typical hummingbird's nest is one of the daintiest structures in the world. Composed largely of softest down from seeds, or of hairs from furry leaves, the tiny cup is prettily decorated on the outside with bits of grayish or greenish foliaceous lichens or with lichens and tufts of green moss. Sometimes lichens also cover the bottom where the eggs lie. Other ingredients of hummingbirds' nests are brown scales from the unrolling fronds of large ferns, fine fibrous rootlets, bast fibers, fragments of grass or leaves, wool, small feathers, and similar materials. Some nests are composed chiefly of green moss, with a downy lining.

Whatever they may be, the materials of a hummingbird's nest are in most cases firmly bound together by liberal amounts of cobweb—the indispensable cement of avian architects—which also fastens the nest to its support. Frequently the rim of the little downy chalice is incurved, reducing the danger that the eggs will be shaken out by wind. These nests are usually situated in trees or shrubbery, either high or low. Some hummingbirds, including the violet-headed in Costa Rica and the giant in Chile, prefer to build on a branch overhanging a stream or other body of water. Others find protection for their nests beneath the projecting top of a streamside or roadside bank or in an Andean cave. Using regur-

Black-throated Mango
(*Anthracothorax nigricollis*)
Northern South America

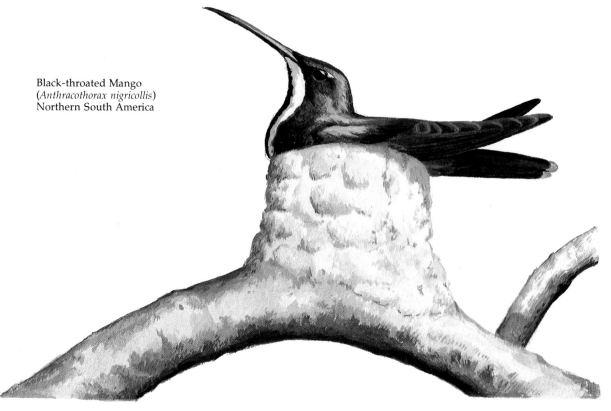

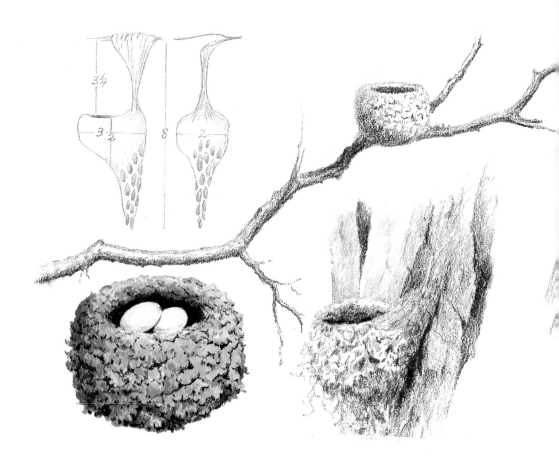

gitated nectar or perhaps saliva as glue, the Andean hillstar attaches its exceptionally large, well-padded nest to a projection on the face of a cliff on the bleak Peruvian puna, usually one that faces east and catches the earliest warming rays of the rising sun.

Hermit hummingbirds fasten their nests beneath a living leaf that forms a green roof above them. Such sites offer no support for perching; when a hermit starts to build, she must work wholly on the wing. Bringing a weft of cobweb, she wraps it around the leaf tip by slowly floating around it on rapidly beating wings, one, two, or three times, always facing it. Then she fastens fragments of vegetation to the cobweb until she has a little shelf projecting from the inner side of the leaf tip, on which she rests while she shapes the mass into the form of a cup or concave bracket that will hold her eggs. The finished structure is often an inverted cone with a hollow in the top and a long "tail" of fibers, shriveled leaves, and other bits of vegetation dangling below the tip of the leaf.

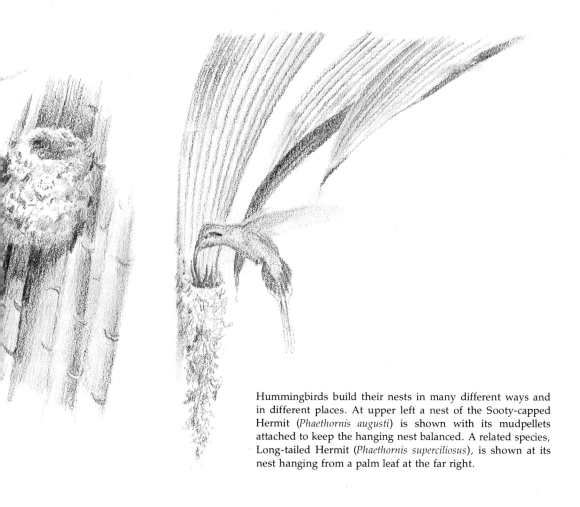

Hummingbirds build their nests in many different ways and in different places. At upper left a nest of the Sooty-capped Hermit (*Phaethornis augusti*) is shown with its mudpellets attached to keep the hanging nest balanced. A related species, Long-tailed Hermit (*Phaethornis superciliosus*), is shown at its nest hanging from a palm leaf at the far right.

Some hermits, including species of *Phaethornis*, build thick-walled nests of soft materials. Others, such as the bronzy hermit and the band-tailed barbthroat, use thin, rather stiff rootlets and leafless stems of mosses and liverworts, making loose, open walls through which much light passes. The advantage of such a structure is that it dries more rapidly, the disadvantage, that it provides poor insulation, but this is not a great handicap in the warm lowlands where most hermits live.

One of the most remarkable nests is that of the sooty-capped hermit of Venezuela, which hangs by a single stout cable of spiders' silk from some overhead support. Since the suspension cable is attached to only one point on the rim of the open cup, the latter would tilt strongly if the builder did not take corrective measures. Directly beneath the point of attachment she fastens, also by cobweb, little lumps of dry clay or pebbles, which dangle below the nest's bottom and act as a counterpoise to keep it level. These curious nests have been found beneath bridges, in highway culverts, and hanging from the roof inside dark buildings.

Like other birds, the hummingbird builds with her bill, feet, and breast. She gathers and brings material with her slender bill, which she also uses to poke it down into the nest, to smooth the outside of her cup, and to press the wall inward to her breast, against which she rounds the structure as she rotates to face in all directions. Her feet knead and compact the materials in the bottom; one can rarely see this, but the bouncing movements of her body suggest that this is what she is doing.

Hummingbirds almost invariably lay two tiny, white eggs, which can be distinguished from those of other birds not only by their diminutive size but by their long, narrow form. Among the smallest are the eggs of the calliope hummingbird, averaging 12 by 8 millimeters—about ½ by ⅓ of an inch. The largest are probably those of the giant hummingbird, 20 by 12 millimeters—about ¾ by ½ inch. This biggest of hummingbirds builds a rather typical nest that seems too small for it, and appears frequently to lay only a single egg.

When a hummingbird's nest contains more than two eggs, they were probably laid by two females. This seems to happen most often with hermits, whose conspicuously hanging nests attract each other's attention. Once I found, attached beneath a strip of banana leaf, a band-tailed barbthroat's nest that two females were visiting. In it were three eggs, and a fourth was on the ground below.

Hummingbirds usually lay their eggs early in the morning, the second two days after the first, rarely one or three days after the first. Sometimes they deposit their eggs in a half-finished nest and continue to build it up while they incubate.

Hummingbirds' eggs are often laid during a season when hardly any other birds are nesting. In the highlands of northern Central America hummingbirds breed chiefly in the first half of the dry season, from October to January or February, when the earth is still damp from long months of rain and sunny skies call forth a profusion of bright blossoms. At this season heavy nocturnal frosts are frequent above 7,000 feet, and cold, boisterous winds may blow across the mountains for days at a time. I used to lie in bed, none too warm under all the heavy Guatemalan Indian blankets that I could pile upon myself, and marvel at the hummingbirds incubating their eggs and rearing their nestlings out on the exposed mountain slopes. But cold and wind are no threat to these hardy little birds as long as heat-producing nectar is abundant.

74 Simultaneously with the hummingbirds nest the flower-piercers,

unrelated songbirds that, like the hummingbirds, subsist largely upon nectar and tiny insects—thus emphasizing once more how abundance of food for the young controls the breeding seasons of birds. I found no other birds breeding in the months when hummingbirds and flower-piercers nested; the great majority did so in April, May, and June, when frosts had ceased and seeds and insects were more abundant, but when flowers were fewest and nests of the nectar-drinkers were not found.

As one descends to lower altitudes, nests of hummingbirds are more uniformly distributed throughout the year. Here on the Pacific slope of southern Costa Rica, 2,000 to 3,000 feet above sea level, I have found newly laid eggs in every month, the greatest number in flowery December as the wet season passes into the dry, with another peak of abundance in May, June, and July, the early half of the rainy season. Nests with eggs are fewest in March and April, when the dry season has made its effects most strongly felt, and in September and October, when rains are heaviest. Although two or more of the fourteen species that breed here have been found nesting in every month, different species prefer different seasons. The hermits, with nests roofed by green leaves, rear their families chiefly or only in the rainy months. Species with open, exposed cups breed mainly in the drier weather, although a few, including the scaly-breasted hummingbird and the rufous-tailed, sometimes attend their nests beneath October's deluges.

In other regions hummingbirds behave rather differently. In Trinidad the hairy hermit breeds chiefly in the drier period from January to April, but continues into the rainy months of May, June, and July, as do certain other hummingbirds. At Belém, Brazil, the hairy also nests in the drier weather, which there lasts from May to October. On Volcán Cotopaxi, near the equator, the Chimborazo hillstar nests in its caves throughout the year. In the temperate zones most hummingbirds breed in spring and summer; but in California Anna's hummingbird starts to lay in December or January, sometimes amid frost or snow, and much earlier than any of the other species in that state.

The female hummingbird, who in most species incubates alone, may sit on her eggs by day for from less than a minute to rarely as much as three hours continuously. Absences often last less than a minute and rarely as long as half an hour. Incubating hummingbirds differ greatly in their patience. Some leave the nest only about 10 times per day; others, more mercurial, as many as 110 times. Since most recesses are brief,

Long-tailed Hermit
(*Phaethornis superciliosus*)
Mexico, Central America,
northern South America

hummingbirds usually keep their eggs covered for from 60 to 80 per cent, and sometimes more, of the daylight hours, which is high constancy for such small birds.

They are especially restless around seven or eight o'clock in the morning, when they leave their eggs frequently to bring more down, lichens, or cobweb, even to an already well-padded and well-decorated nest. Except in the cases of nests that were incomplete when the eggs were laid, the chief importance of this activity seems to lie in the constant renewal of the cobweb binding that holds the nest together and fastens it to its support. This is especially necessary in the nests of hermits fastened beneath the tips of slippery leaves. In the afternoon many hummingbirds incubate much more constantly than in the forenoon.

The leafy roof above them forces long-billed hermits, which invariably sit facing the side where the nest is attached, to bend their head back until the crown almost touches the rump, in what appears a most strained, uncomfortable posture. The first time one sees a hermit sitting bent almost double, he pities the bird. Yet she hardly needs our sympathy, for she can maintain this seemingly intolerable flexure for well over an hour; indeed, hermits sit for longer intervals than many other hummingbirds.

As mentioned, while incubating eggs or brooding nestlings, hummingbirds do not become torpid on cool nights. By fixing a thermocouple in an artificial egg and placing it in a nest of a calliope hummingbird in the high mountains of Wyoming, William Calder showed that she could keep her eggs 40° to 54° F above the air temperature on cold nights.

Hummingbirds' eggs take much longer to hatch than the much larger eggs of many songbirds. The incubation period, or interval between the laying of the last egg and its hatching, is, in different species of hummingbirds, generally fifteen to nineteen days. As in other birds, it may be prolonged a few days beyond this by inclement weather that forces the female to stay away from her nest for longer intervals. In a harsh environment the Andean hillstar commonly takes twenty-two or twenty-three days to hatch her eggs. The parent may carry away the papery empty shells or leave them to be crushed into the bottom of the nest.

Hummingbirds hatch in an even less developed state than most songbirds. Ugly, unpromising little grubs, they have tightly closed eyes, mere bumps for bills, and for covering only two rows of tiny down feathers along the center of their back. Most never acquire a downy coat, but remain naked until their pinfeathers burst, to release the plumage in which they will leave the nest.

When the mother comes to feed these nestlings, nothing is visible in her bill, which she pushes so far down into their throats that one who watches the act of feeding for the first time fears for their lives. Then, by rather violent muscular exertion, she brings up the food from her crop and passes it to her little ones. Nearly always she divides the food rather equally between the two of them, regurgitating to each one or more times on a single visit to the nest. As in other birds that feed their young by regurgitation, hummingbirds do so rather infrequently, bringing food to their two nestlings, on the average, from 1.2 to 2.5, or, less often, 3 times per hour, with little increase in the rate as they grow older. After a generous meal the nestlings' necks are grotesquely swollen where the crammed esophageal pouch protrudes on the right side.

DURATION OF INCUBATION AND PARENTAL CARE

Hummingbird	Locality	Incubation Period	Nestling Period	Last Feeding Seen at Days
		In Days	In Days	
			From Hatching	
Band-tailed Barbthroat	Costa Rica	18½−19	24−25	56
Hairy Hermit	Para, Brazil	16	22	
Little Hermit	Costa Rica	15−16	20−23	
Scaly-breasted	Costa Rica	17−19	22−26 (29)[1]	65
Green Violet-ear	Mexico, Costa Rica	16−17	23−25 (28)[1]	
White-eared	Mexico, Guatemala	14−16	23−26 (28)[1]	40
Rufous-tailed	Central America	15½−16	19−23 (27)[1]	58
Blue-throated	Mexico	17−18	24−29	
Andean Hillstar	Peru	22−23	30−40	
Long-billed Starthroat	Costa Rica	18½−19	25−26	48
Anna's	California	16	25−26	
Costa's	California	16−18	20−23	

[1]nestlings' development retarded by inclement weather.

At first the mother hummingbird broods her young at frequent intervals; but when they are only eight to twelve days old, and still rather naked, they are left to pass the night without the maternal coverlet. As Calder and others have shown, at twelve days they have already developed a fair measure of temperature control and, in a snug downy nest, can keep their tiny bodies many degrees warmer than the night air. On high tropical mountains the mother may cover her nestlings by night until they are considerably older and well feathered; female white-ears do so until the nestlings are seventeen or eighteen days old.

Strangely enough, a daytime shower may send a mother hummingbird to cover nestlings that have been sleeping exposed to the nocturnal sky, even on wet nights; and when hot sunshine beats upon them, she may stand on the nest's rim to shade them. But nestling hummingbirds are amazingly hardy, surviving exposure to rain and strong sunshine and even falls that would be fatal to the nestlings of many other small birds.

While the nestlings are very tiny, their mother throws their droppings from the nest with the tip of her bill, swallows them, or carries them away. When they are older, they rise up and shoot their waste over the rim. While still only blind, naked grubs, hermit hummingbirds orient themselves with their heads toward the sheltering leaf and their posterior ends outward, just as their mother incubates and broods. This orientation, which they maintain until they fly, permits them to eject their excreta clear of the nest without soiling the supporting leaf. Thus hummingbirds' nests are at all times kept clean.

As the two nestlings approach their mother in size they become crowded in a cup that was molded closely around her body, but the downy nest now stretches to accommodate their growing bodies. Sometimes they burst it asunder. Then they may either fall to the ground or remain resting on the flattened platform.

Hummingbirds sometimes try to help at a nest that is not their own. In Mexico Helmuth Wagner saw strange females feed both nestling and fledgling white-eared hummingbirds. If the mother finds such a helper at her nest, she chases her away. Once he saw a green violet-ear feed young white-ears. In Ruschi's aviary a female planalto hermit adopted sixteen-day-old nestlings whose mother had died, attending them as though they were her own.

When about sixteen days old, most young hummingbirds are fairly well clad in plumage and have quite outgrown their infantile ugliness. Bright-eyed, alert young creatures, they look around with interest, preen their fresh plumage, and from time to time rise up to beat their wings vigorously, holding on to the nest to avoid being lifted from it.

These wing exercises seem necessary for the young birds' development, and it is important that the nest be so situated that they can be done without striking a wing against anything. While two nestling bronzy hermits were growing up beneath a banana leaf, it began to dry and fold around them like a tent. The nestling on the left side had enough room to flap its wings freely and left when about three weeks old. The young bird on the right, lacking space to spread its right wing fully, formed the habit of exercising with this wing partly folded. After the young hermit had delayed in the nest almost a week too long, I tried to help it by pushing out the disturbing leaf with a long pole. This made it flutter to the ground. Its right wing was raw and bloody; it could not fly; and despite continued maternal attention, it did not survive.

Few hummingbirds fly undisturbed from the nest before they are three weeks old, and nestling periods of twenty-four or twenty-five days are

Broad-tailed Hummingbird (*Selasphorus platycercus*) Western U.S., Mexico, Guatemala

not unusual. Inclement weather may retard their development and pro-
long their life in the nest by several days. Raised in a rigorous environment,
the Andean hillstar lingers in the nest for the exceptionally long period
of thirty to forty days. Unless frightened, hummingbirds, like most other
birds, leave the nest quite spontaneously, with no parental urging. Usually
they depart in the morning. Since the female often starts to incubate
before she lays her second egg, one nestling may hatch a day or so
before the other and likewise leave the nest a day or two sooner. From

80

the first, hummingbirds fly well, sometimes covering fifty feet or more on their first attempt.

Black-chinned hummingbirds in the southwestern United States continue to be fed by their mother for at least two weeks after they leave the nest. As in tropical birds of other families, tropical hummingbirds may attend their young much longer, sometimes for a month after nest-leaving. A scaly-breasted hummingbird continued to be fed for forty-one days after it took wing, or until it was sixty-five days old. Juvenile hummingbirds do not follow their foraging parents in the manner of many other birds, but they do have a special place where their mother comes to feed them. If the young bird is absent when its parent arrives, she may perch in the trysting place and call. Days before two young long-billed starthroats achieved independence, they became mutually antagonistic, and one tried to prevent its brood-mate from being fed.

Just as other juvenile birds learn to choose their food by trial and error, sometimes sampling objects as indigestible as bits of bark, so hummingbirds may try at first to suck nectar from a pale red leaf, or something else that in color or shape resembles a flower. By such exploratory probing they learn where to find food. The tendency to explore persists into adult life and leads them to new sources of nectar.

Hummingbirds often rear two broods in a season, sometimes laying again in the same nest, sometimes building a second nest above the first, to make a two-story structure. Some northern species show their great vitality by building a new nest, and even laying eggs and starting to incubate, while still feeding nestlings in their first nest, as has been recorded of the Anna's hummingbird, the rubythroat, and the related black-chinned hummingbird. I have not known a tropical hummingbird to be occupied with two nests simultaneously, but a female white-ear built a rather flimsy second nest and incubated in it while still feeding a juvenile from her first brood.

Although in nearly every species that has been carefully studied at the nest only the female has attended it, from time to time one reads of a male hummingbird that helped. Most such reports are based upon rather casual observation. Perhaps the most thorough study of a nest attended by two adults was that made in the mountains of Venezuela by Ernst Schaefer, who photographed a male and female sparkling violet-ear sitting by turns on the same set of eggs. Although among violet-ears the sexes are usually quite alike, this male could be distinguished by his abnormally light crown. After alternating with the female in incubation, he helped feed the single nestling that hatched. His attendance at this nest continued for at least sixteen days.

We cannot exclude the possibility that the behavior of this male was abnormal, like his plumage. No less of an authority than Augusto Ruschi has denied that male sparkling violet-ears assist at the nest; in Ecuador he watched a free female incubate alone, and in his aviary two females reared five broods without masculine help at any stage. Yet Ruschi has stated that males of the hermit genera *Glaucis* and *Phaethornis* usually cooperate with the female in caring for the young, which is contrary to my own experience with representatives of these genera. Recently, in California, Mrs. Dale Clyde watched an Anna's hummingbird in adult male plumage repeatedly feed a feathered nestling whose mother had just vanished; but such attentiveness is surely exceptional in this well-known species.

Although I have never seen a male hummingbird build, incubate, or feed nestlings, I have found one species in which the male's association with a female is more than transitory. For the past six years a female bronzy hermit has nested on this farm, in a small banana plantation bordered by old forest and tall second-growth thickets. Possibly she was always the same individual, as her nests, attached to strips of banana or wild plantain leaves, were all in neighboring sites. For at least four of these years a male was closely associated with her and spent much time perching at the edge of the nearby thicket or in a coffee bush almost below her nest. From time to time he flew up to inspect it, and frequently he escorted or chased the female as she left or returned. During the period of construction he occasionally sat in or circled around the nest, in the motions of building, although I never saw him bring any material to it.

His chief occupation was driving away intruding hummingbirds, including other female bronzy hermits, who are very troublesome at certain nests. He stayed with the same female throughout the nesting season, even when this was prolonged by the loss of successive nests. Perhaps he remained mated to her year after year, as in many other families of tropical birds.

Enemies and Friends

SOMETIMES I HAVE WATCHED a hawk pass overhead while, with shrill notes, a hummingbird flew close above or beside it, like a little fighter plane buzzing a huge bomber. To keep watch over the movements of foes, to know exactly where they are and what they are doing, is sound military practice that birds commonly follow, hummingbirds no less than larger kinds. Often a motley crowd of small birds gathers around a resting raptor or snake, flitting nervously and complaining or scolding in a medley of voices. In the tropics hummingbirds are often present in these gatherings, and, as in the case of the flying hawk, they may approach closer to the enemy than other birds dare. One day, while I walked through the forest, a commotion in the treetops drew my attention to a spectacled owl, sitting somnolently on a high limb with feathers all puffed out, making it appear huge. Trogons, honeycreepers, and hummingbirds were mobbing the owl. The little hummingbirds approached closer than the others, almost touching it with their bills.

In defense of their nests, hummingbirds are surprisingly bold, attacking with spirit, and often putting to ignominious flight, birds and mammals much larger than themselves. In Trinidad Collingwood Ingram saw a white-chested emerald buffet with audible wing blows a great kiskadee, one of the most powerful of the flycatchers, that had approached too near her nest. I have watched a scaly-breasted hummingbird drive from

83

Hummingbirds are famous for their courage in defending their nest. This pair of Velvet-purple Coronet (*Boissonneaua jardini*) found in Colombia and Ecuador are chasing an Ornate Hawk Eagle (*Spizaetus ornatus*).

her nest a blue-diademed motmot many times her size. A calliope hummingbird, the smallest feathered creature in the United States, pursued a squirrel through the trees until it was far from her nestlings. The hummingbird's usual procedure is to threaten the intruder with menacing darts, again and again, until it retreats; only rarely does she strike it, and apparently never with her bill, which is too fragile to be used as a weapon. Other hummingbirds do not attack or threaten an intruder, but complain incessantly when nest or young are, or appear to be, in danger.

Despite their great maneuverability in the air, hummingbirds are occasionally surprised and captured by hawks. I have never myself seen a raptor—or anything else—catch an adult hummingbird, but others have reported instances of this. It seems to be the smaller, more agile hawks that succeed in stealing up unseen and seizing the unsuspecting hummer. Ernst Mayr saw a sparrow hawk capture a ruby-throated hummingbird at a bed of zinnias. Hans Peeters watched a sharp-shinned hawk catch a perching Anna's hummingbird by approaching near the ground,

screened by bushes, until within striking distance. Larger raptors appear more rarely to prey on hummingbirds, but the remains of a rubythroat were once found in a pigeon hawk's stomach. Even more surprisingly, a male Baltimore oriole seized and killed a male ruby-throated hummingbird that was hovering in front of the same flowers the oriole was probing.

Sometimes the hummingbird is surprised by an attack from a quarter where it can hardly expect it—from below. While a hummingbird visits low flowers, a large frog may leap up from amid the herbage and engulf the bird in its capacious mouth. While a migrating female rufous hummingbird drank at the brink of a lake, a frog jumped out of the grass, knocked her into the water, then seized her and carried her into the submerged vegetation. Also in California, a bass leaped up and swallowed a hummingbird that hovered above a lotus pool.

Hummingbirds may even fall victims to insects, the larger of which exceed them in size. In September, 1948, two ruby-throated hummingbirds were seized by praying mantises while visiting blossoms, one in Pennsylvania and the other in Texas. In each case, a woman who was watching promptly tried to rescue the bird. The hummingbird in Texas survived; the one in Pennsylvania was killed by the insect's stubborn grip. Occasionally, dragonflies pursue and even seize ruby-throated hummingbirds, perhaps mistaking them for territorial rivals. In Ontario a huge dragonfly caught a hummingbird by the neck and was holding it on the ground when the timely arrival of some people drove the insect away and saved the bird's life.

Among the hazards of hummingbird life are becoming entangled in spiders' webs and stuck to prickly flower heads. Whether while gleaning insects from the webs, gathering silk for their nests, or simply flying carelessly, hummingbirds are sometimes caught in a large, tough spider's web, where they may hang helplessly until they die if somebody does not rescue them. Occasionally, the spider, if large, proceeds to wrap her avian prisoner in a shroud of silk before sucking its blood, as she does with her insect victims.

A male ruby-throated hummingbird was so closely stuck to the head of a purple thistle that he could not fly until released by human hands. In Idaho a calliope hummingbird, who lacked such timely succor, was found dead, firmly attached by its feathers to a spike of bristly foxtail grass. Large birds, including black-capped chickadees, yellowthroats, and pine siskins have been caught by the hooks on the flower heads of common burdock, and doubtless this fate sometimes befalls hummingbirds too.

Window glass and screens take the lives of many birds. They are especially hazardous when they are situated so that birds can see trees or shrubbery through them, as through opposite windows of a room. Expecting to reach the leafy boughs that they plainly see, the birds try to fly through the room, only to hurl themselves against the treacherously invisible windowpanes or the scarcely more visible fine-mesh wire netting. Stunned by the impact, they fall to the ground, perhaps to die. Unlike larger birds, the hummingbird often rams its needlelike bill into a mesh so hard that it cannot release itself.

I recall a dwelling in Honduras with a narrow projecting porch, screened on three sides, that was a deathtrap for the hummingbirds that visited the surrounding fruit trees. If promptly freed by gently pushing their bills outward, some of those caught in the screen flew away, apparently not much the worse for their experience. But half an hour of motionless hanging beneath a hot tropical sun, with tightly constricted bill, was fatal.

Too late we found their glittering, dehydrated bodies stuck to the screen. So many hummers and other birds fly through the rooms of our home near the tropical forest that to prevent distressing tragedies, our windows are wholly unobstructed, except when closed by wooden shutters.

Although small and difficult to detect, the nests of hummingbirds fare no better, and perhaps even worse, than those of other birds of the same region; in only a minority of them do the young remain safely until they can fly. The causes of loss appear to be much the same as in other small birds. In the first hummingbird's nest that I ever studied, on a Panamanian plantation, week-old nestlings were killed by fire ants, which continued to swarm over the corpses until only tiny bones remained. Snakes, small mammals, and nest-robbing birds, such as jays and toucans, probably pillage many a nest, although one rarely catches them in the deed. I suspect that bats, certain kinds of which are known to prey on birds, plunder nests of hermits fastened beneath the tips of slippery palm fronds, where they seem out of reach of most creatures that cannot fly and where predatory birds are much less likely to find them.

Even at high altitudes, where predators, especially snakes, are fewer than in teeming tropical lowlands, nesting hummingbirds have poor success. Among woods of oaks and pines around 8,500 feet in Guatemala I found nine white-eared hummingbirds' nests, in which eighteen eggs were laid. Nine eggs hatched, but only three of the young survived to fly. Similarly high nest losses have been noticed in other regions. Since the annual mortality of hummingbirds appears to be low, they need raise few young in order to maintain their population.

That birds form personal attachments can hardly be doubted by the naturalist in the tropics, who sees many kinds flying two by two throughout the year, even when the nesting season is months away and their reproductive urges are dormant. But hummingbirds are different. Their social impulses are minimal, and except in a few species, their association with a partner of the opposite sex lasts only long enough to ensure that the eggs will be fertilized. How unexpected, then, to discover that at least some hummingbirds are capable of responding to the friendship of the man or woman who provides sweet nourishment for them.

During the year that the artist Arthur Fitzpatrick lay sick in a Californian sanatorium, he had a feeder hung outside his bedroom window, where he could watch the feathered visitors. After the usual skirmishing, a male rufous hummingbird won firm possession of it as his "feeding territory" and spent much of his time there, sipping syrup and chasing away intruders.

The presence of a creature so brilliant and full of vitality, so indomitable in the defense of his feeder, cheered the invalid, gave him an outside interest, and hastened his recovery. When at last Fitzpatrick was permitted to go outside in a wheelchair, the rufous left the feeder to zoom around his benefactor's head, then poise in front of each lens of his eyeglasses, as though in friendly greeting. Even when the glasses were removed, the hummingbird hovered before the man's eyes; it was not his own reflection in the spectacles that attracted him. When the convalescent finally returned home in a car, the rufous somehow followed to his house, eight miles away.

Then, to build up his strength, the artist began daily walks, on which the hummingbird always accompanied his human friend, flying ahead and perching until the slower pedestrian caught up. Observant and curious, the rufous, by hovering before whatever interested him, called his companion's attention to much that, alone, he might have overlooked: once a family of quail chicks with their strutting parents, once seven baby skunks, once a large rattlesnake lying half-hidden in the path. After his full recovery Fitzpatrick returned to his work in the city, and a month passed before he could revisit the mountains. Yet seconds after he alighted from his car, the rufous was there, whizzing around his head and dancing back and forth before his glasses.

This, which reads like a fairy tale, yet rings true, is about the best hummingbird story I know. I can believe it more readily because the rufous hummingbird's attachment to the man who fed him seems a further development of that personal recognition of the provider of syrup that Althea Sherman had noticed in her ruby-throated hummingbirds long before; and I myself have had a bicolored antbird who would fly up whenever he saw me in the forest and follow me closely for long distances, catching the insects that I stirred up from the undergrowth and ground litter. The remarkable part of this story is that the rufous was apparently not fed on his walks with the artist, although he doubtless visited flowers and caught insects along the way. He seemed to accompany the man because he liked his company.

The Past and Future of Hummingbirds

OF THE ORIGIN OF HUMMINGBIRDS in the distant geological past, we can only vaguely speculate. Some have suggested that the ancestor of the family was a swift or swiftlike bird that took to gleaning insects from flowers, found nectar in them, became increasingly addicted to this sweet nourishment, and in the course of many generations evolved into the efficient nectar-drinker that the hummingbird is. Certainly this hypothetical ancestor of hummingbirds was totally unlike contemporary swifts, which catch their insects while flying high in the air and take no interest in flowers or nectar, which their very short bills and tongues are poorly fitted to exploit. Possibly the anatomical similarities of hummingbirds and swifts, especially their wings that are nearly all "hand," are an example of evolutionary convergence, the process by which organisms of quite different ancestry come to resemble each other in structure when they adopt similar modes of life. Both swifts and hummingbirds have evolved extraordinary powers of flight, which they use in wholly different ways.

A more promising approach to the origin of hummingbirds is to seek it in some bird of long ago with habits somewhat like those of modern honeycreepers: a bird with a slender bill and a fondness for nectar, but with such rudimentary ability to hover that it probes flowers while perching or clinging and, not being an efficient nectar-drinker, depends largely upon fruits and insects. Many birds ill-fitted for procuring nectar are,

89

nevertheless, eager for it. I have watched short-billed tanagers and finches obtain it by pulling off tubular corollas and biting their bases to press it out, or by probing the calyxes or stumps of the corollas for the sweetness that remained there. Although the hummingbird family is usually classified with the nonpasserine birds, certain students have placed it in the passerine order. It may well be that it had a passerine ancestor.

Although we cannot tell the ancestry of hummingbirds, we can answer another question of great interest: Why are there so many kinds of hummingbirds? Why is this the second-largest family of exclusively New World birds?

In the first place, the hummingbird system of reproduction promotes relatively rapid evolutionary change. In monogamous birds a male begets no more offspring than he and his single mate can rear. In the hummingbird system a male with some attraction that wins many temporary partners can sire a much greater number of progeny. Some of them may receive his advantages—his ornamental plumage or more compelling courtship display—in intensified form, becoming, in turn, fathers of many nestlings. In the course of generations this process leads to both amplification and diversification of the characteristics by which female hummingbirds recognize appropriate nuptial partners. On a smaller scale, we witness the same phenomenon among the less numerous manakins of the New World and birds of paradise of New Guinea and Australia, which have, mostly or wholly, mating systems similar to that of hummingbirds.

In the second place, relatively rapid species formation has been favored in hummingbirds by great adaptability. Not only are they very abundant in warm tropical lowlands, they have also been able, thanks to their ability to conserve energy by noctivation, to follow flowering plants up to the highest altitudes where they can grow, on the verge of the snow that crowns the highest Andean peaks. Few other families of birds do this. Some species of hummingbirds have become specialized for life in the lower levels of tropical rain forest, others high in the trees; some have adapted to arid regions; some take readily to man's gardens and plantations; a few, becoming long-distance migrants, have extended the range and increased the diversity of the family. The isolation afforded by deep, trenchlike Andean valleys has helped to multiply species. Some kinds of hummingbirds are confined to single valleys; others have an immense range, from Mexico to Bolivia.

It has been said that hummingbirds are so successful because they have exploited an ecological niche, a possible mode of life, neglected by other animals, and so have reduced restrictive competition. It would be truer to say that hummingbirds are so successful because they have created the niche that they occupy. When their remote ancestors began to visit flowers, they must have been in full competition with insects, earlier sippers of nectar and carriers of pollen. After primitive hummingbirds proved that they, too, could pollinate flowers, plants responded, in an evolutionary sense, by creating floral forms better fitted for hummingbird than for insect pollination. As these forms became more diverse, hummingbirds changed with them, until now we find a great variety of bills adapted to visiting different kinds of flowers. This has also increased the number of species in the family. In a similar way, frugivorous birds have created their own ecological niches: after they proved their value as disseminators of seeds, flowering plants competed for their services, producing a variety of fleshy fruits to attract and nourish them.

What of the future of hummingbirds? Today, everywhere in tropical America, where the great majority of hummingbirds live, the natural vegetation, especially forest, is shrinking at an appalling rate before a too-rapidly expanding human population. With the destruction of their habitat, hundreds of species of birds face extinction. Some, including hummingbirds, have possibly already vanished, never again to grace it with their presence, no matter how many eons our planet continues to support life.

In the face of this distressing menace, hummingbirds appear to have a better prospect for survival than many birds more narrowly adapted to tropical woodland, such as toucans, trogons, and antbirds. Some species, at home in the deep forest or with a narrow range, may disappear. But hummingbirds are adaptable, and many will doubtless persist, perhaps retreating to inaccessible ravines, whence they will at intervals sally forth to gather nectar in neighboring cultivation. Some species, indeed, are benefited by the spread of agriculture, irrigation, and the multiplication of human homes surrounded by flower gardens. This has happened to such successful hummingbirds as the Anna's in California, the rufous-tailed in Central America, and others elsewhere.

Meanwhile, before it is too late, we would like to know a great deal more about the family that Robert Ridgway has called "the most charming element in the wonderfully varied bird-life of the Western Hemisphere, but, also, without doubt, the most remarkable group of birds in the entire world." The naturalist with the enterprise and hardihood to study living hummingbirds in Andean puna and páramo, montane forests, and shrinking Amazonian selvas will surely enrich natural history with some fascinating discoveries.

As one finishes a survey of the hummingbird family, he continues to ask: Why does it contain so many exquisite gems? "Because their glitter helps to intimidate rivals," some students of bird behavior would say. But does beauty arouse fear? "Because the display of their adornments stimulates the female to accept the male," is the answer that Darwin's theory of sexual selection offers. But can the female distinguish and appreciate all the adornments of one of the more elegant male hummingbirds as he darts swifty before her? Probably neither of these answers is wholly wrong, yet they hardly seem adequate. To have a satisfactory explanation of hummingbirds' loveliness might deepen our understanding of this so enigmatic universe—and of ourselves.

Elicia's Hummingbird (*Hylocharis eliciae*)
Mexico, Central America

BIBLIOGRAPHY

The Hummingbird Family— General References

Bent, A. C. *Life Histories of North American Cuckoos, Goatsuckers, Hummingbirds, and Their Allies.* U.S. Natl. Mus., Bull. 176, 1940. Reprinted by Dover Publications, New York, 1964. (Habits and distribution of hummingbirds of the United States and Canada; illustrated.)

Gould, J. *Monograph of the Trochilidae.* London, 1861, 2nd. ed. and supplements 1880–1885. (Superb illustrations of most species.)

Greenewalt, C. H. *Hummingbirds.* Garden City, N.Y., Doubleday and Co., 1960. (General account, with original research on flight and coloration; color photographs.)

Meyer de Schauensee, R. *A Guide to the Birds of South America.* Wynnewood, Penn., Livingston Publishing Co., 1970. (Brief descriptions and ranges of 233 species; colored figures of some.)

Ridgway, R. "The Humming Birds." U.S. Natl. Mus. Rept. for 1890, 1891, pp. 253–383. (A general survey; illustrated.)

Ridgway, R. *Birds of North and Middle America.* U.S. Natl. Mus., Bull. 50, 1911, Part V. (Generic diagnoses, detailed descriptions and measurements of all species of the North American continent and West Indies.)

Ruschi, A. *Observations on the Trochilidae.* Bull. Museu de Biol. Prof. Mello-Leitao, Santa Teresa, E. E. Santo, Brazil, 1949. (Portuguese, mimeographed translation made for C. H. Greenewalt; a broad survey of behavior, especially in an aviary.)

Scheithauer, W. *Hummingbirds.* Trans. by G. Vevers. New York; T. Y. Crowell and Co., 1967. (Behavior in aviary, flight, feeding, etc.; color photographs.)

Wetmore, A. *The Birds of the Republic of Panama.* Smithsonian Miscl. Coll., 150, Part 2. Smithsonian Institution Press, 1968. (Descriptions and behavior of fifty-four species.)

Colors and Adornments

See references for Chapter *The Hummingbird Family* especially Greenewalt and Ridgway, 1891.

Flight

Blake, C. H. "The Flight of Hummingbirds." *New England Naturalist,* No. 3 (1939), pp. 1–5.

Pearson, O. P. "Speed of Allen Hummingbird While Diving." *Condor,* 62 (1960), p. 403.

See also references for Chapter *The Hummingbird Family* especially Greenewalt and Scheithauer.

Food, Metabolism, and Longevity

Bartholomew, G. A., Howell, T. R., and Cade, T. J. "Torpidity in the White-throated Swift, Anna Hummingbird, and Poor-will." *Condor,* 59 (1957), pp. 145–155.

Lasiewski, R. C. "The Energetics of Migrating Hummingbirds." *Condor,* 64 (1962), p. 324.

Lasiewski, R. C. "Oxygen Consumption of Torpid, Resting, Active, and Flying Hummingbirds." *Physiological Zool.,* 36 (1963), pp. 122–140.

Lasiewski, R. C., and Lasiewski, R. J. "Physiological responses of the Blue-throated and Rivoli's Hummingbirds." *Auk,* 84 (1967), pp. 34–48.

Morrison, P. "Modification of Body Temperature by Activity in Brazilian Hummingbirds." *Condor,* 64 (1962), pp. 315–323.

Pearson, O. P. "The Metabolism of Hummingbirds." *Condor,* 52 (1950), pp. 145–152.

Pearson, O. P. "Use of Caves by Hummingbirds and Other Species at High Altitudes in Peru." *Condor,* 55 (1953), pp. 17–20.

Pearson, O. P. "The Daily Energy Requirements of a Wild Anna Hummingbird." *Condor,* 56 (1954), pp. 317–322.

Pearson, O. P. "Torpidity in birds." In *Mammalian Hibernation.* Bull. Mus. Comp. Zool. Harvard, 124 (1960), pp. 93–103.

Scheithauer, W. (Reference in Chapter 1.)

Sherman, A. R. *Birds of an Iowa Dooryard.* Boston, Christopher Publishing House, 1952. (Chapter 16.)

Van Riper, W. "Sugar for That Slim Girlish Figure." *Nature Mag.,* 46 (1953), pp. 135–136, 162.

Bills and Tongues, Flowers and Insects

Bené, F. "The Role of Learning in the Feeding Behavior of Black-chinned Hummingbirds." *Condor,* 47 (1945), pp. 3–22.

Bené, F. 1946. "The Feeding and Related Behavior of Hummingbirds with Special Reference to the Black-chin, *Archilochus alexandri*" (Bourcier and Mulsant). Mem. Boston Soc. Nat. Hist. 9 (1946), pp. 403–478. (Twelve plates.)

Collias, N. E., and Collias, E. C. "Anna's Hummingbirds Trained to Select Different Colors in Feeding." *Condor,* 70 (1968), pp. 273–274.

Foster, W. L., and Tate, J., Jr. "The Activities and Coactions of Animals at Sapsucker Trees." *Living Bird,* 5 (1966), pp. 87–113.

Grant, K. A., and Grant, V. *Hummingbirds and Their Flowers.* New York, Columbia Univ. Press, 1968. (Thirty color photographs.)

Miller, R. S., and Miller, R. E. "Feeding Activity and Color Preference of Ruby-throated Hummingbirds." *Condor,* 73 (1971), pp. 309–313.

Pitelka, F. A. "Territoriality and Related Problems in North American Hummingbirds." *Condor,* 44 (1942), pp. 189–204.

Skutch, A. F. "Scarlet Passion-flower." *Nature Mag.,* 45 (1952), pp. 523–525, 550.

Snow, B. K., and Snow, D. W. "Feeding Niches of Hummingbirds in a Trinidad Valley." *Jour. Animal Ecol.,* 41 (1972), pp. 471–485.

Verbeek, N. A. M. "Hummingbirds Feeding on Sand." *Condor,* 73 (1971), pp. 112–113.

Vuilleumier, F. "Field Notes on Some Birds from the Bolivian Andes." *Ibis,* 111 (1969), pp. 599–608.

Wagner, H. O. "Food and Feeding Habits of Mexican Hummingbirds." Wilson Bull., 58 (1946), pp. 69–93.

Wolf, L. L. "Female Territoriality in a Tropical Hummingbird." *Auk,* 86 (1969), pp. 490–504.

Daily Activities and Temperament

Stoner, E. A. "Anna Hummingbird at Play." *Condor,* 49 (1947), p. 36.

Weydemeyer, W. "Injured Calliope Hummingbird Lifted by Another." *Auk,* 88 (1971), p. 431.

Courtship, Voice, and Nesting

Banks, R. C., and Johnson, N. K. "A Review of North American Hybrid Hummingbirds." *Condor,* 63 (1961), pp. 328.

Barash, D. P. "Lek behavior in the Broad-tailed Hummingbird." Wilson Bull., 84 (1972), pp. 202–203.

Calder, W. A. "Temperature Relationships and Nesting of the Calliope Hummingbird." *Condor*, 73 (1971), pp. 314–321.

Clyde, D. P. "Anna's Hummingbird in Adult Male Plumage Feeds Nestling." *Condor,* 74 (1972), p. 102.

Cogswell, H. L. "Alternate Care of Two Nests in the Black-chinned Hummingbird." *Condor*, 51 (1949), pp. 176–178.

Davis, T. A. W. "The Displays and Nests of Three Forest Hummingbirds of British Guiana." *Ibis*, 100 (1958), pp. 31–39.

Dorst, J. "Etude biologique des trochilidés des hauts plateaux Péruvienes." *L'Oiseau et R. F. O.*, 26 (1956), pp. 165–193.

Dorst, J. "Nouvelles recherches biologiques sur les Trochilidés des hauts Andes Péruviennes (*Oreotrochilus estella*)." *L'Oiseau et R. F. O.*, 32 (1962), pp. 95–126.

Hamilton, W. J., III. "Sun-oriented Display of the Anna's Hummingbird." Wilson. Bull., 77 (1965), pp. 38–44.

Howell, T. R., and Dawson, W. R. "Nest Temperatures and Attentiveness in the Anna Hummingbird." *Condor*, 56 (1954), pp. 93–97.

Nickell, W. P. "Alternate Care of Two Nests by a Ruby-throated Hummingbird." Wilson Bull., 60 (1948), pp. 242–243.

Pitelka, F. A. "Breeding Seasons of Hummingbirds near Santa Barbara, California." *Condor,* 53 (1951), pp. 198–201.

Schäfer, E. "Sobre la biologia de *Colibri coruscans*." Bol. Soc. Venezolana Sci. Nat., 15 (1954), pp. 153–162.

Skutch, A. F. "The Life History of Rieffer's Hummingbird (*Amazilia tzacatl tzacatl*) in Panama and Honduras." *Auk*, 48 (1931), pp. 481–500.

Skutch, A. F. "Life History of the Violet-headed Hummingbird." Wilson Bull., 70 (1958), pp. 5–19.

Skutch, A. F. "Life History of the White-crested Coquette Hummingbird." Wilson Bull., 73 (1961), pp. 5–10.

Skutch, A. F. "Life Histories of Hermit Hummingbirds." *Auk*, 81 (1964), pp. 5–25.

Skutch, A. F. "Life History of the Scaly-breasted Hummingbird." *Condor*, 66 (1964), pp. 186–198.

Skutch, A. F. *Life Histories of Central American highland birds.* Cambridge, Mass. Nuttall Ornith. Club, Publ. No. 7, 1967.

Skutch, A. F. *Studies of Tropical American Birds.* Cambridge, Mass., Nuttall Ornith. Club, Publ. No. 10, 1972.

Smith, G. T. C. "A High Altitude Hummingbird on the Volcano Cotopaxi." *Ibis,* 111 (1969), pp. 17–22.

Snow, D. W. "The Singing Assemblies of Little Hermits." *Living Bird*, 7 (1968), pp. 47–55.

Wagner, H. O. "Notes on the Life History of the Mexican Violet-ear." Wilson Bull., 57 (1945), pp. 165–187.

Wagner, H. O. "Beitrag zur Biologie des Blaukehlkolibris *Lampornis clemenciae* (Lesson)." Veröff, Mus. Bremen, Reihe A, Bd. 2 (1952), pp. 5–44.

Wagner, H. O. "Versuch einer Analyse der Kolibribalz." Zeit, f. Tierpsychologie, 11 (1954), pp. 182–212.

Wagner, H. O. "Beitrag zum Verhalten des Weiss-sohrkolibris (*Hylocharis leucotis* Vieill.)." Zool. Jahrb. Syst., 86 (1959), pp. 253–302.

Wiley, R. H. "Song Groups in a Singing Assembly of Little Hermits." *Condor*, 73 (1971), pp. 28–35.

Wolf, L. L., and Wolf, J. S. "Nesting of the Purple-throated Carib Hummingbird." *Ibis,* 113 (1971), pp. 306–315.

Enemies and Friends

Bent, A. C. (Reference in Chapter 1.)

Fitzpatrick, A. "My Friend Rufous." *Florida Naturalist*, 39 (1966), pp. 35–38, 54.

Mayr, E. "Hummingbird Caught by Sparrow Hawk." *Auk,* 83 (1966), p. 664.

Morgan, M. "Hummingbird Killed by Frog." *Condor*, 59 (1957), p. 69.

Norris-Elye, L. S. T. "Leopard Frogs Devouring Small Birds." *Auk*, 61 (1944), pp. 643–644.

Peeters, H. J. "Two Observations on Avian Predation." Wilson Bull., 75 (1963), p. 274.

Tucker, H. M. "Caliope Hummingbird Entangled in Grass Barbs." *Condor*, 57 (1955), p. 119.

Wright, B. S. "Baltimore Oriole Kills Hummingbird." *Auk*, 79 (1962), p. 112.

INDEX